A PARENTS PRIVILEGE

RAISING CHILDREN
– a parents privilege –

David and Liz Holden

KINGSWAY PUBLICATIONS
EASTBOURNE

First published 1995

Unless otherwise indicated, biblical quotations are from the
New International Version, © 1973, 1978, 1984 by the
International Bible Society.

ISBN 0 85476 595 6

Design and layout by Pinnacle Creative Ltd for
KINGSWAY PUBLICATIONS LTD
Lottbridge Drove, Eastbourne, E. Sussex BN23 6NT.
Printed in Great Britain,
by arrangement with Bookprint Creative Services.

This is dedicated to the many parents whose family life has been an excellent example to Liz and me.

Acknowledgements

Firstly, we would like to thank all at Sidcup Community Church who have continued to work out the values shown in this book with consistency. Your families are a joy to be with.

Secondly, thanks to Carol Harris, my personal assistant, who has worked so hard and patiently (as always) in helping to put this book together.

Contents

Liz and I have both been involved in producing this book, although it may seem that I've been the main contributor. The reason for this is purely practical — to make the book easier to read. We agree on what's being said, but it often sounds less complicated if only one of us says it.

Foreword

Increasing numbers of people are giving up on marriage. The responsibility of raising children is regarded as daunting. Many have thrown away old guidelines, but have found no replacements. They are often in a sea of bewilderment, disappointment and even fear of the future.

How refreshing it is, then, to find David and Liz Holden's book presenting clear, practical guidelines on raising children in the modern world. They are unashamedly biblical in their approach, fully confident that for the best results you follow the Maker's instructions. Many couples will be helped and encouraged by taking this teaching seriously, and many children will thank God that their parents bothered.

David and Liz are well qualified to write on this theme. They've both been raised in godly homes and they've spoken at seminars on the theme at such places as Stoneleigh Bible Week. Their own children are a delight and totally vindicate their parents' convictions and practices.

I wish this fine book every success.

Terry Virgo

PART 1

Children:
judgement
or joy?

CHAPTER 1

Introduction

There are many reasons why raising children is such an important subject. The first and most obvious is that it's become one of the greatest needs in our society today. A couple who have been born again and filled with the Spirit don't suddenly have children who are magically transformed overnight. They've lived with a worldly philosophy for many years and their children have lived with it too. There's no point saying to them, 'Just raise your children as the Bible teaches' because they don't know what it teaches. They've got to start from scratch. They need training in how to bring up their children according to God's Word.

The Bible says, 'Sons (daughters) are a heritage from the LORD, children a reward from him' (Ps. 127:3). Children aren't here to ruin our lives. They're gifts from God. He wants them to be a joy and it's our privilege to raise them as well as we can. Maybe you're a parent, or thinking about having children. What does God want you to produce in these children? The way you raise them will reveal whether you think they just exist or have a purpose in coming into your life.

Sometimes children who are supposed to bless us actually threaten to finish us off! We want them to enhance our lives, but they cause us tremendous anxiety and we almost end up wondering if we should have had them in the first place. I'm sure none of us would say that, but rearing children can be incredibly stressful, as any parent will know.

So the next time you're with your children at a mealtime and they're doing things they shouldn't do and you're gritting your teeth, remind yourself of Psalm 127. And say in your heart, 'You're a gift from God, a wonderful heritage. I'm so glad that you have come into the world to bless my life and the lives of all the other people around us as well.'

Many of us have read books or been to seminars on the topic of raising children and we feel inadequate as parents. It's good to be honest, to say at times, 'We don't think we've got it right. We want to learn again.' I often do that. I haven't 'arrived'. I'm constantly watching others, talking to parents who've got more experience than I have, asking, 'How do you manage your children? How did you learn to do that?'

Some couples concern me. They think that because they've read the book, seen the film, heard the tape — somehow that's it. But they're actually on a constant learning curve. Parents can never say, 'We've arrived. We're now perfect parents with perfect children and there's nothing else to learn.' Jesus said that those whose lives are built on the rock are not just hearers of the Word, but doers as well. It's not, 'How much do you know?, but 'How are you doing?'

My greatest reason for writing this book is this: I believe that a christian family can be one of the greatest evangelistic tools that God can use in society today. Family life is falling apart around us and a christian family is a fantastic testimony. Naturally, we don't tell our friends and neighbours, 'Our family life is terrific because we're christians'. We say, 'It's God, not us. He's teaching us from His Word and we're living by it. He's involved in our family life and making it work.' Christians should be able to lead the way in showing the world what family life is all about, because if you take God out of families you remove the reason for their existence.

There's a world out there that has huge questions and is desperate for the answers. People are longing to know how to raise their families in the best way. God is longing for christians who will show them. He wants you to receive His grace and help and to see how powerful your witness can be to those who live around you.

Today there are many christian books on raising children, but hardly any from a British perspective. I hope, therefore, that you will be able to feel closer to the scene that I'm describing. When there are references to biscuits, it really does mean biscuits and not 'cookies'!

Also, for our American brethren, the word smack in the UK means the same as their word spank. It doesn't mean to beat up, which the word smack means in the USA. I discovered this rather belatedly when I once spoke on raising children in Washington DC.

Society offers us many different and confusing ideas which clamour for our attention. We desperately need the wisdom to know which way to go — particularly when it comes to raising children. The Bible says, 'The fear of the LORD is the beginning of wisdom' (Prov. 9:10). Wisdom is about honouring God and His Word. So if you want to be wise in the way you raise your children, you don't gather the latest psychological information. You read the Bible and live by it.

Christians need to battle through on this. We must question our basis for family life. Is it a women's magazine or the Word of God? We're God's children, new creations in Christ, and we live in a new Kingdom. So we shouldn't be surprised if unbelievers are offended by our behaviour. They're actually screaming for something different. We're different and will raise our children differently from them.

In the 1960s many psychologists, doctors and child care experts began to write books. These books were based on secular humanism and drew people further and further away from the Word of God. 'This is how you should raise your children' they said. 'Reason with them. Give them freedom of expression.'

Many of the people who wrote these books have since rewritten them. They've looked back over two decades and seen the fruit of their ideas. And they've said, 'We got it wrong. Look at our society, our young people. There's disruption everywhere.' The tragedy is the rewritten books aren't being read by the people who devoured the original ones. We're still building our educational system on things that haven't worked, and our whole society reflects the so-called freedom of the 60s.

Liz and I have four children: Emily, Daniel, Lucy and Julia. They're completely different but the same principles apply to all of them, although in each case they may be worked out in a different sort of way. Needless to say, we've made many mistakes and we're still learning. That should encourage you, because you're bound to be in the same boat.

CHAPTER 2

The state of
our nation

If we were living in a society where everyone out there was getting it right, we would have to say, 'OK, you teach us then. We'll learn about family life from you.' But people in the world aren't getting it right, so it's pointless our following their example. There's only one alternative and it's with God. We must come back to His Word because that's where the answer lies.

In the 70s and early 80s everyone was frightened by the threat of nuclear war. People are still fearful that a bomb will fall in their back garden, but they don't notice that there's a bigger bomb already exploding underneath them. It's been there for a long time, sending shock waves though society, causing marriage breakdown, rejection of children and confusion everywhere. The core of society is breaking down and the family unit is probably under a greater threat than ever before.

There are more divorces in England than in any other country in Europe. There are more single parents and abandoned children. There's probably more child abuse — although that's hard to quantify because no one used to talk about it and now it's coming out into the open.

Then there's the 'children divorcing parents' phenomenon. I understand that there's a queue of 14, 15 and 16 year-olds who want to divorce their parents. Leaflets are now given out at school gates to 1st and 2nd year pupils at senior schools instructing them on how they can find legal aid to take their parents to court. In one issue of *Just 17* magazine there was a free insert on your rights as a child to divorce your parents. I can think of many children who will take that very seriously.

Now that we've advanced in embryonic and genetic selection, people are questioning the role of the father. He can plant the seed, as it were, but is there any need for his ongoing involvement from there on? That's tragic — an issue that should never even be considered.

Then there's a huge pressure to go along with the crowd. One example of this concerns women with small children who are encouraged to return to work. Now I haven't got a 'thing' about this. My concern is simply for the women who don't want to go back to work. The trouble is that they're so pressurised to conform that they feel like second class citizens if they stay at home to look after their little children.

Sometimes I turn on the television in the mornings and see one of those dreadful chat show programmes — agony aunt things. If you're like me, you're sitting there screaming, shouting at the television, almost throwing things at it and getting in a complete stew because you're thinking, 'This is NOT the answer! These people really don't know what they're talking about.'

God didn't plan chaos for the family. It was never His intention for marriages to break down, for children to be rejected, or for the family unit to fall apart at the seams. He is *for* the family, and has been from the beginning. His Word tells us that He 'sets the lonely in families' (Ps. 68:6). This verse alone tells us that God is committed to the family unit. Clearly, if family life is breaking down, God must be having a hard time finding families to put the lonely into.

Family life is not an inevitable hassle. Marriage is not about making it through. It's a wonderful provision of God. Children are not a punishment. They're God's gifts to parents. God wants children to be raised in a secure atmosphere, knowing their parents' love and His direction. If we follow His plan for family life, we'll make it through in the end.

CHAPTER 3

A challenge

If society is falling apart and family life is being eroded, then there's a challenge for every christian couple: do we raise our children according to the philosophy of this world, or according to the Word of God?

This world's philosophy is built on something called secular humanism, which states that we can manage on our own and therefore have no need of God. This opposes the teaching in the Word, which states that God is the source of everything. He is the creator who made men and women and instituted marriage and family life. If something's going wrong, we must get back to God and to His blueprint in the Word.

Many christian couples don't raise their children according to God's Word. 'The world has got some good ideas' they say. 'We're going to investigate them further.' Certainly unbelievers can teach us some valuable lessons on child rearing, but our basic foundation must be the Word of God. No one can force you to raise your children by the Bible. You must make that choice yourself.

It is important to make a clear decision about this, because if you choose to go down this line you'll be in the minority. Your beliefs about raising children will offend people and they may laugh at you, or even refuse to speak to you. There's a cost involved, but it's worth counting because God's way is the only way that works. You'll go through hassle and pain, but at the end of the day you'll have great children. Other parents will look at the results and will wonder how you did it. And you'll tell them that this is what happens when you build your family life on the Word of God.

Our children don't decide whether they're going to be raised according to secular humanism or the Word of God. That's up to their parents. We must take full responsibility for the way we bring up our children. We're the key to what they become.

I often think that the issue is more about raising parents than raising children. You see a child who is really causing hassle in the church or the street and you're tempted to think, 'Wretched child. He's got so many problems.' But behind that young person there's a parent. If you see a child misbehaving, don't just blame him, ask where the parents are. And remind yourself that if you want to raise your children well, you've first got to be a good parent.

In his book, *Raising Positive Kids in a Negative World*, Zig Ziglar says,

> *The only way to raise positive children is to start by being a positive parent, and the positive parent is the one who makes decisions right at the beginning — this is how we're going to raise our children, these are the standards we're going to have, this is where I'm going*

to take my basis, my foundation of the way my family will be produced'. He also says, 'Take control early or lose control for ever'.

Raising Positive Kids in a Negative World by Zig Ziglar, © Thomas Nelson.

A friend of mine teaches twelve and thirteen year-olds and when he can't control one of them, he calls in the parents. Usually they tell him, 'We can't do anything with our son/ daughter. It's your responsibility.' Clearly they've already given up and the poor teacher is left to manage a rebellious child who's never been taught the difference between right and wrong. The responsibility lies firmly with us as parents — which may sound a daunting prospect. The good news is that if we take the task seriously, God will be with us and will help us through.

In the midst of all this darkness and depression, God is building His church and is raising up parents who will take His Word seriously. The Bible promises us that He will 'turn the hearts of the fathers to their children, and the hearts of the children to their fathers' (Mal. 4:6). That's what we're believing God for — restoration. If you play your part, your children won't shame you, they'll be a joy.

It's embarrassing to see parents publicly caught out — at the school gate for example, when their children's behaviour puts them to shame. If you raise your children according to God's Word, the promise is that they will honour you and not put you to shame. It may take time, but your goal should be to be able to say, 'If we go there, I know that they'll behave!'

Before I go on, I just want to say that I'm conscious that there will be single parents reading this. My main focus will be the family unit, but I want single parents or divorcees to be encouraged too. I also want unbelievers to learn from the principles that we're going to share. I've taken some family life seminars where unbelieving husbands were present. They've listened to what I've said and have gone out and applied the teaching, only to find that it works. So if you have non-christian friends, don't hesitate to pass this book on to them. It will certainly lead to some interesting conversation.

CHAPTER 4

Training

What will cause your children to be the greatest joy for you — rather than a sort of judgement or condemnation? It's this: positive training. Children won't be a joy to you unless you train them — it's a God-given principle. It's also something that both parents need to do together. Some husbands think their wives should do the training. I utterly refute that! Mothers and fathers have the joint responsibility of training their children.

Children aren't born trained. Actually, the only thing they're trained to do is sin. Have you noticed that? You don't need to tell your four year-old son, 'This is how you hit your two year-old sister over the head with a toy car!' Sin comes naturally — it's just there.

Someone once said, 'It's better to build children than repair men'. I like that. Children's formative years are crucial for their future. And training is the key. The Bible says, 'Train a child in the way he should go, and when he is old he will not turn from it' (Prov. 22:6). This is a much quoted verse, but there are actually many other Scriptures that make parents responsible for training their children.

So whether you like it or not, if you're a parent, you're a trainer. It's a tragic mistake to let your children find their own way. God doesn't want to see your children born and abandoned. He wants you to train them to grow up in His ways and to be responsible for their actions. It's your God-given responsibility. Don't neglect it.

The word 'train' in the phrase, 'Train a child in the way he should go' is used in the context of breaking in a horse. A wild horse needs to be harnessed and given direction. In the same way we need to set boundaries for our children and teach them to obey us. Children who have no boundaries, instruction or direction don't know whether they're coming or going.

Some parents have adopted a modern philosophy which suggests that children can live in a sort of vacuum. 'We mustn't impose anything on our children,' they say. 'Rather, we must let them express themselves and do what they like.' They think that if you start training your children, you're crushing their personalities and putting them down. But godly training never puts people down. It always brings them through to maturity.

Let's be honest. If you don't train your children, someone else will. It may be the television or other parents. It may even be the children in the playground at school. Children are easily influenced. You watch them! Peer pressure starts long before they're thirteen years old. There's a constant stream of influence flowing in their direction. Atheistic new age parents are training their children in their philosophy.

And vegetarian parents are bound to be telling their children why they don't eat meat. That's training. How much more then should christian parents take up their responsibility to train their children in the ways of God? Here are five things you need to help you to do this:

1. The grace of God. In no other area do I need the grace of God more than in the raising of four children. I need grace to admit my mistakes to them and to understand why they're like they are. I'm constantly dependent on God's grace to give me the ability to raise them well.

2. The Holy Spirit. It amuses me to hear people say, 'I need the Spirit's power to witness, to perform signs and wonders, to heal and cast out demons'. I agree with them. But I also need the Spirit to raise four children. The Spirit is interested in how we raise our children and He doesn't want us to do this alone. He's there to instruct and help us. As we're constantly filled with the Spirit, He will help us to train our children to be godly and wise.

3. The Word of God. We've touched on this already and will come back to it later.

4. Vision. You need to have hopes for your children's future. I'm not talking about university and career, but about the sort of people you want them to be — how you want their characters to develop. You must have some sort of goal in this area, or else you'll never know where you're headed, nor will you be able to measure your success. Each child is unique, God has made them individuals. As a parent you are looking with keen interest, not only to see, but also to help that individual to fulfil their full potential.

5. More experienced people. It is not a sign of weakness to ask for advice on how to raise your children. Before Liz and I had children, we didn't have a clue about raising them, but we wanted to do God's will. So just before Emily was born we talked to other parents and bled them dry of everything they knew. We were so grateful for their help.

Because I travel quite a lot, I often spend time in people's houses. It's been a privilege to arrive in some homes and to have the parents say to me, 'Look, while you're here we'd like you to look over our family life. If there's anything you notice about our marriage, or the way we're raising our children, please feel free to comment on it.' It's challenging for parents to do that. They usually wait until you're about to leave before they give you this kind of invitation!

Christians are so privileged. We're not out in the world struggling on our own to keep on top of family life. We have so many resources — God's grace, His power, His Word, vision and godly people who are more experienced than we are.

The challenge I want to bring to you is this: your spiritual state reflects the way that you raise your children. I was once talking to a guy who was backsliding. We were chatting away about the effect that his backsliding would have on his life and I said, 'What about your family?' He replied, 'Well, it won't affect my children. It's got nothing to do with them.' But it has. I've watched parents who have neglected their relationship with God and I first see its effects in their children. Almost immediately, their children's attitudes change. It's a great challenge to walk continually in the power of the Spirit and to stay close to God.

CHAPTER 5

Train them to know God

I want to give you two reasons why we should train our children. I'll deal with one in this chapter and the other in the next. Here's the first reason: so that they'll get to know God personally and learn more about Him. Paul says, 'Fathers, do not exasperate your children; instead, bring them up in the training and instruction of the Lord' (Eph. 6:4). When we train our children, we're showing them who God is and what He's like.

Our lives should reflect the character of God to our children. We tell them that God is a God of love and righteousness and they are not confused. Rather, they immediately respond, 'Of course He is!' Why? Because they see His love and righteousness in our lives. We don't teach them the latest ideas, or even our own ideas. We teach them the Word and back that up by our lifestyle.

This sort of training won't just result in well-behaved children, it will ensure that they want to know God too. I've tried to point my children in the right direction. From an early age they all knew about God, but I always made sure that they were clear about one thing: they didn't know Him for themselves.

That's the first thing I want my children to grasp: that they aren't christians because they've been born into a christian family. When they've got revelation of that, they realise that there's an area of need in their lives. They know that they're not going to make it because you're their parents. They're going to get through because, like you, they recognise that they're sinners who need to be saved.

All four of our children have made clear commitments to Jesus that came out of a time of knowing that they needed to be saved. Before they became christians I felt quite happy to say, 'You're not ready yet.' Some christian parents think that they can't do that. They want to get their children saved by the time they can say 'Dada' and 'Mama!' But we shouldn't be afraid of giving our children space to know that they aren't born again and to ask questions about what this means. You want clear conversions. Your children need to know about God and about their need of God. You have the privilege of training them so that they reach the place where this decision can be made.

It's a fantastic advantage to be brought up in a christian home, although many people don't think so. They tell you, 'I was brought up in a christian family. I've got a boring testimony. If only I'd had a time of rebellion.' Well, I had a christian home and I feel sorry for those who didn't have this privilege. You may have had a good old fling before you got saved, but I didn't and it's never worried me. The funny thing is that the people who 'went wild' before they came to Christ are saying, 'I wish I'd been brought up in a christian family like yours'.

Paul says that it's an advantage to be a Jew because Jews are near the words of God (Rom. 3:1,2). This means that they might come to God quickly. So tell your children that it's a great advantage to be brought up in a christian home because they're nearer to the Word of God, through which they can be born again.

Psalm 78 begins, 'O my people, hear my teaching; listen to the words of my mouth. I will open my mouth ...' That's how you train people — you open your mouth and speak. You tell your children about God's greatness and about His wonderful Word. The Psalm continues, 'I will open my mouth in parables, I will utter hidden things, things from of old — what we have heard and known, what our fathers have told us. We will not hide them from their children; we will tell the next generation the praiseworthy deeds of the LORD, his power, and the wonders he has done. He decreed statutes for Jacob and established the law in Israel, which He commanded our forefathers to teach their children, so that the next generation would know them, even the children yet to be born, and they in turn would tell their children. Then they would put their trust in God and would not forget his deeds but would keep his commands. They would not be like their forefathers — a stubborn and rebellious generation, whose hearts were not loyal to God, whose spirits were not faithful to him'.

I'm staggered when christians don't speak to their children about God — His works, His Word, His power, the church and signs and wonders. I give my children a regular diet of church history. They're amazed by the lives of Wesley and Whitefield and learn all about revivals. At bed time I've read them stories about the Welsh revival and they sit there and think it's wonderful. They say to me, 'But Dad, it's like most of my class being saved.' And I reply, 'That's right. And I believe that one day this could happen in your generation. Wouldn't that be great?'

I'm teaching them that christianity as we know it isn't the full expression of what it could be. I want them to get a sense of what's happened in the past, what's happening now and what God may want to do in the future. It's great to tell your children about these things and to get them involved. We'll talk more about this later. My point for now is that we should teach our children about God and help them to understand their need of Him. This isn't the school teacher's responsibility — even if it's a christian school, and it isn't just the responsibility of the church. God calls you, the parents, to train your children in this way.

CHAPTER 6

Train them to reach the world

The second reason why we should train our children is this: so that they can stand up for themselves and reach their generation for Jesus. All our training is for this purpose: that they might take on the world. The Bible says, 'Like arrows in the hands of a warrior are sons born in one's youth. Blessed is the man whose quiver is full of them. They will not be put to shame when they contend with their enemies in the gate' (Ps. 127:4,5).

When the psalmist was declaring this truth, arrows weren't mass manufactured. Every warrior had his own arrows which he individually made and sharpened. You're the warrior, involved in a battle for truth. Your children are the arrows in your hands. While the battle rages on, you're fashioning your children, preparing them to go out and take ground for Jesus. They're going to change the direction of the battle and alter the society in which they live. All your training is for their maturity. You want your children to grow up thinking and acting for themselves according to the Word of God.

If you're still having to hold your child's hand when he or she has reached the age of eighteen, something's gone wrong somewhere. You don't want them to remain immature but to know how to do things for themselves. You're training them to give them away, not to keep them. So you must make sure you do a good job while you've got them because they won't be with you for long.

Discipleship never keeps people under, it always exalts them and prepares them for something. While we must protect our children, we mustn't over protect them. We're not keeping them from the world, we're preparing them to take on the world. It's not a fearful thing but a glorious privilege.

I have four potential world changers in my home. It's up to Liz and me to train them according to the Word of God. That's a different way to look at children and at how you relate to them, isn't it? It's almost guaranteed to change your view of motherhood because investing yourself in world changers doesn't sound exactly second class. So what sort of people are going to change the world? Let me give you six things that you can build into the lives of your children.

1. Security. The world is full of insecurity. We must train our children to be secure in who they are and in everything that's going on around them. We must play our part by making sure that our love for them never changes, that it is always constant and for them, frequently expressed with affection and words. If they never have reason to doubt your love they will always feel secure. When people see individuals who are secure, they'll take note and be amazed.

2. Emotional balance. Our emotions are a healthy part of our make-up — they are God given. We need to make sure that

we do not suppress our emotions but easily express our feelings and train our children to feel comfortable in expressing theirs. It is far better to allow emotions to have an outlet, and if they need correcting, to correct them, than not to have any freedom to express feelings at all.

Children should be full of life and bounding with energy — they need to know that life with Jesus invades every area of family life and is not just confined to church meetings. Otherwise we are in danger of producing spiritually weird children. They should be emotionally well-balanced and happy. So when they're older and all their friends are trying to 'find themselves', they don't have this problem. That's because they've been brought up in an environment where they've already 'found themselves'. They're emotionally secure and well-balanced. And they love life.

3. Confidence. We must train our children to have a certainty about their lives. We need always to be available to encourage them to persevere and to praise them constantly for their achievements, however small. We don't want them to be easily shaken, but to have a deep inner confidence.

4. Respect for authority. Children must be taught to have a basic respect for authority — both your authority and also the authority that underlies the whole of society. I'm utterly convinced that teachers at school are on the receiving end of the huge neglect of parents training their children. The nation is mystified by children killing other children. You cannot just look at those children, questions need to be asked about the parents too.

5. Truth. People who are full of truth can oppose the lies of the enemy. Our children will be fighting battles in their

generation that we haven't fought in ours. We must ensure that truthfulness and honesty are the norm at home. We must always speak the truth and teach our children to have respect for the truth. Once lying starts it becomes a habit that's very hard to break, so we must always deal with it immediately and explain how serious it can become if allowed to grow. We must teach them the truth so that they can overcome the pressures that they and their children are going to face in the future.

6. Destiny. Hope, purpose and destiny — so many children (and teens) ask, 'Why am I here?' Our goal is that each child has a real part to play in life. They are not drifting aimlessly through life. They were born for a purpose — it's even good to build that sense of destiny into young children. They are going to make a difference in their world. Of course their real destiny can only be fulfilled in knowing Jesus and living to please Him.

So who will take on and change the world? People who are secure, emotionally balanced, confident, respectful of authority, full of truth and conscious of their destiny. All of these characteristics are missing in society today. If we build them into our children, we'll see a generation of young people grow up and take on the world.

CHAPTER 7

Faith and example

The Bible says, 'without faith it is impossible to please God' (Heb. 11:6). We don't just need faith for things like healing and provision, we need it for our children too. Without faith for them, we won't please God. You can face the task of raising your children with fear and foreboding, or with faith.

Jesus said, 'In this world you will have trouble. But take heart! I have overcome the world' (John 16:33). You're not training your children to keep their heads above water in the world. You're training them to take on the world. For that, you need faith that they'll be able to make it through.

Although there's a sense in which your children belong to you, there's another sense in which they don't. They really belong to God and He's lent them to you. That's a good way to see it, because it helps you to keep them in an open hand and stops you becoming too possessive. Many children are trying to get free from over possessive parents, some of whom could even be christians.

It's great to say, 'Lord, I give my children to You'. Then if they respond to an appeal to go to the ends of the earth, you won't panic and think, 'All these years of training and they want to serve the Lord in Outer Mongolia. I was hoping that they'd get married, have children and live round the corner from me'. Well, they're not yours, they're God's. You just train them up and by faith you let God do with them whatever He wants to.

I sometimes talk to parents who are full of despair and negativism about their children. They automatically expect the worst — particularly as their children approach their teenage years. But we mustn't think like this. We must be full of faith. It's faith that declares, 'We've raised them according to the principles of God's Word and we've talked things over. We've got faith for them when they face difficulties, peer pressure and temptations. We're trusting that they'll overcome because God will bring them through.'

The Bible character, Daniel, was only about fifteen when he was removed from his family and taken to a foreign land. I've often wondered who his parents were and how they coped with this separation. I believe they'd done a good job on him because when he arrived in Babylon, he was clear about what he had to do. Our children may go away from us at times — maybe even to foreign lands. As we wonder how they're coping, we must have faith that what God's Word says is as true for them as it was for us. We got through. They're going to get through as well. And all our training is to that end.

BE AN EXAMPLE
We've already touched on this, but there's no greater way of training children, than by setting an example. Zig Ziglar says,

'Being effective parents hinges on trust. If kids know that their mum and dad believe what they are teaching and if kids know that what their parents teach is consistent with the life they live, then kids will trust their parents and will respond positively to what their parents say. Hypocrisy, if it ever was in, is totally and completely out with children today. We fail our children if we say don't do as I do, but do as I say'. Ibid.

We're failing our children if we ever tell them to do something that we're not doing ourselves. We need to give them a good example to follow.

So there you are, Mum and Dad. Your children are with you and they're doing something. You look at each other and one of you says, 'Where does she get that from? How did he learn to do that?' And they sort of smile at you because they know very well where they got it from. Now hopefully what they're doing is positive, but it need not be — it depends on the influence that you're having on their lives. They're watching every move that you make, listening to every word that you say. You've heard the phrase, 'a chip off the old block'? Well, you rub off on them — in a positive or a negative way.

Liz:
It is important that we don't translate our own background into a fear that the same thing may happen to our children. I had some negative experiences as a child. Through knowing Christ I was wonderfully set free from these, but when I had my own children a fear arose that it might happen to them. When I looked at my husband's trust and faith for them, I realised I was being dominated by a lie and I had to replace the fear

with faith. This gave me confidence to believe God and to trust Him for them. It also made me secure and confident when I talked to the children. Don't allow past negative experiences to dominate your thinking and make you fearful and over protective. Come through and find faith for yourself and your children.

It's sad how many children who are brought up in christian families rebel because of the lack of consistent example. 'Mum and Dad behave in this way on Sunday morning' they say, 'but the rest of the week they're different.' They see what everyone else doesn't.

So on Sunday you, the parents, have a disagreement, you're late for church, one of the children sticks their finger in the door which you slam shut because you're in a hurry. The children are screaming, arguing and fighting in the back and you arrive at the car park. 'Good morning' you say to someone. 'Hallelujah! Praise God!' You can fool this person that everything's fine, but not your children. They see the hypocrisy, and the greatest way to train them is to be a consistent example to them all the time.

One reason why children are often negative is because their parents are negative. If they grumble and complain, it's because they've heard you doing it. You can tell them not to grumble and if they're small, they can't answer you back. But when they're bigger, it's a different matter. If you get angry and raise your voice, they'll raise their voices because they're watching you. If you lack self control, so will they. How can you tell your child to do what you're not doing? How can you complain that your son is lazy and watches too much television if you're always in front of the box? You can't have it both ways. You set the standard.

Some people tell me, 'The real problem is, I'm just a useless parent'. Then they pass the buck onto someone else. There's an awful lot of surrogacy going on in the body of Christ. I often find myself playing the role of a surrogate husband or parent. When that happens I think, 'Hold on! Why am I doing this? I've got four of my own! You've got to deal with this yourselves!'

God has given your children to you. They don't need any other parents. You're no mistake. You're unique, the best they could have! And God has given you all the resources you need to bring them up. You may think you're a useless parent, but there's no such thing. You're a child of God, a new creation, a citizen of the Kingdom. Ask God to change, instruct and help you. Don't just go through life thinking everything will turn out all right in the end. Cry out to God every day. 'Lord, make me a better father, a better mother. I need You.' Yes, you may fail from time to time, but you've got to come back to God and find confidence from Him that you can set an example.

CHAPTER 8

Attitudes

I've already mentioned that our children don't come trained. They have wrong attitudes that need to be corrected. I want to be very practical and give you some negative attitudes that need to be detected and trained out of our children. Then I'll give you the positive attitudes which need to replace them.

WHINING OR EXCESSIVE CRYING

Whining — 'I don't want to' — and excessive crying is all about one thing: manipulation. A child thinks, 'I'm going to manipulate my parents into letting me do something and I'm going to win in the end'. You must deal with this. If you let them whine when they're young, what will they be like when they're older? The opposite to whining is cheerfulness. Train your children to be cheerful.

SOUR FACIAL EXPRESSIONS

When children realise that they can't get one over you by whining and crying, they'll just pull a face. And they may be rude when people visit, refuse eye contact when they're spoken to, or sulk when they're told off. When my son Daniel was disciplined, his first reaction was to pull a face. We'd find him outside in the hallway sulking with a sour expression. This is an attitude problem which we must deal with.

The opposite to sulkiness is joy and friendliness. One of our children is very shy, but there's a thin line between sulkiness and shyness. I've got to detect which is which. I don't mind children being shy if that's part of their nature. But there's no excuse for sulkiness and sour facial expressions. My children may be shy, but they're going to be friendly. They're going to look you in the eye and communicate. I'm training them in that way.

PHYSICAL EXPRESSIONS

Let's start with stamping your feet. We all know about this because we've done it in the past. Then there's sighing. When they're older you hear a 'tut' as they're going out of the door. 'Pardon Daniel? Please clear up the breakfast table.' 'Tut. Do I have to?' Or maybe you reach out to take your child's hand but he jerks it away. Here's another one: your kid throws himself on the floor, kicks his feet in the air and stamps on the ground. Parents explain this away, 'Our child has tantrums' they say. Well, this may sound strange, but we are fortunate that our children don't have temper tantrums. This is because we have always tried to nip such behaviour in the bud. Don't let the 'stamping feet stage' even begin! You don't have to tolerate this kind of behaviour. You can train them in the opposite quality — self-control.

DISRESPECTFUL TONE OF VOICE

When they get a bit older, their tone of voice can become loud, bemoaning or sarcastic. The opposite traits are respect and honour.

SELFISHNESS

A child is naturally selfish. This is expressed in the desire always to be first, a reluctance to share toys with any of their friends and an unwillingness to let life rotate around anyone else apart from them. Sometimes parents don't help. If you're an over doting parent, you're going to make them even more selfish. And if one of their grandparents is over doting, your kids are going to have extra attention and will become selfish all the time. Service is the opposite to selfishness. Teach them from a very young age to serve and to share.

GRUMBLING AND COMPLAINING

This is usually detected in the repeated word, 'Why?' The opposite is gratitude. You stop them from grumbling and train them to have a grateful heart.

UNWILLINGNESS TO SEEK FORGIVENESS

Children emphatically protest their innocence even when it's obvious that they're guilty. Everyone knows the truth, but the kids will insist that they're innocent even to the point of downright lying. The opposite of this is humility. We need to train our children that it isn't a weakness to say 'sorry' and ask for forgiveness.

We mustn't just detect negative attitudes in our children. We must train them to develop positive attitudes. It's really practical. Now, on to a few thorny issues.

POLITENESS

Your children must learn to be polite. It isn't some sort of English thing to teach your child to say, 'please', 'thank you', 'excuse me' or 'may I?' It's good for your children to learn to be polite because they learn other things as well.

When Lucy was given a cake at a friend's house, I said to her, 'Lucy, what do you say?' She looked at the person who had given her the cake and wouldn't answer. I repeated the question. Then I took her into another room, talked to her and brought her back. The lady gave her the cake again. 'Lucy' I said, 'what do you say?' This went on and on and in the end she said, 'Thank you'. Breakthrough! Marvellous! Wonderful! The heavens rejoiced and the angels came! Then when she'd eaten the cake she asked politely, 'Can I have some more please?' You must never allow them to say a stark, 'No'. It's always, 'No thank you', 'No Daddy', or 'No Mummy'.

Some children try to cut across adult conversation. There you are at the end of a Sunday meeting, people are serving coffee and everyone's chatting. You're talking to someone and suddenly there's this child tugging at your leg. 'Yes, just a minute' you say. And they reply, 'But Dad ...' and cut right across your conversation. You must train them to wait patiently and respect you.

Table manners are important too. Children should be grateful for their food and thank the person who made it or gave it to them. They should also sit properly and stay at the table. If they want to be excused they should ask first. This is training.

THOROUGHNESS OR NEATNESS
Children must learn to put away the things they've been playing with and to keep their bedrooms tidy. When you train your kids to do this, you're actually teaching them a principle which has much broader repercussions. It's about finishing the projects that they begin — and you must be their example in this.

OPENNESS

Telling the truth is always vital and however firm you are on this in your home the school playground, in particular, is a training centre for not doing so. My children became quite 'gifted' in the area of lying or half truths. You have to work hard at this one in order to counter the peer pressure your children are under, but your 'high' standards will win in the end. Never allow anything but the truth to win, compromise in this area will have disastrous consequences.

LOVE

Your children must learn how to feel and express love without shame. This is really important, particularly if you were brought up in a family where love wasn't expressed much through words and touch. You make sure that the same won't be true in your family. Most English families don't express love enough — it's time to be expressive!

DISCIPLINE

It's important that your kids accept discipline willingly. We'll talk about this in more detail later. For now, they need to accept it because they know that it's the right thing.

CREATIVITY

Train your children to be creative. There are many books, both christian and secular, that can feed you with great ideas on how to help our child be more creative. I want my children to enjoy creative activities and in an era of, 'just watch the TV', it takes more effort on our part than ever before.

SERVICE

You must teach them how to look for ways to help and serve others. This is especially true in the home, but also among their friends and your friends too.

Parenthood is a wonderful privilege and responsibility. Let me encourage you to remember the phrase that we mentioned earlier: 'It is better to build children than to repair men.' Please don't take this teaching on training children from me alone. Check it out with others whom you respect. Ask them questions. Glean information. Let them help you to become even better parents than you are now.

PART 2

Love and discipline:

a contradiction?

CHAPTER 9

Love and discipline: a contradiction?

People in society would often like us to believe that the answer to this question is, 'Yes'. It seems that either you go with one or the other. But child raising isn't about love or discipline. It's about both. Discipline isn't an isolated subject, which is why it must never be separated from the sort of teaching that I've already shared with you. It's part of a much wider package. So let's look at the question: 'Love and Discipline: a Contradiction?' Clearly the answer is 'No, not at all'.

The motivation behind discipline is love. There certainly isn't any other reason why we should discipline our children. The Bible says, 'My son, do not make light of the Lord's discipline, and do not lose heart when he rebukes you, because the Lord disciplines those he loves, and he punishes everyone he accepts as a son. Endure hardship as discipline; God is treating you as sons. For what son is not disciplined by his father? If you are not disciplined (and everyone undergoes discipline), then you are illegitimate children and not true sons. Moreover, we have all had human fathers who disciplined us and we respected them for it. How much more should we submit to the Father of our spirits and live! Our fathers disciplined us for a little while as they thought best; but God disciplines us for our good, that we may share in his holiness. No discipline seems pleasant at the time, but painful. Later on, however, it produces a harvest of righteousness and peace for those who have been trained by it' (Heb. 12:5–11).

The reason why God disciplines us is because He loves us. In fact, discipline is a proof of His love (v. 6). You know that you're a son of God because God disciplines you. Even Jesus was disciplined. He 'learned obedience from what he suffered' (Heb. 5:8). Without discipline adults and children will question whether or not they are really loved.

Parents are called to train their children in many different areas, and discipline is an important part of this training. It involves more than smacking your children. It's about letting them know the boundaries — the rules of your home and then ensuring that those house rules are kept.

Your rules may be different from mine. Some parents let their children leap all over the furniture and virtually pull it to pieces. Other parents don't tolerate this sort of thing. Suppose you allow your children to trample over the furniture and they go to a home where they're not allowed to do this. And suppose the parent there says, 'Excuse me, don't jump on the sofa'. If your children have learnt the principles of discipline, they won't turn around and declare, 'But we're allowed to in our home!' They'll accept what that parent says straight away. The result of discipline isn't perfect behaviour — we'll never achieve that. It's obedience. You make sure than when you tell your children to do something, they do it.

A friend once shared an interesting insight with me. He told me that he noticed that his children were naughty and that they continued to be naughty — a remarkable revelation! But he learnt something important from this. He said that children could be naughty, but could also be obedient. I don't mind naughty children. They're born that way. But they must also be obedient. Your naughty three year-old may be just about to run into a busy high street. You cry out 'Stop!' and however naughty he is, he obeys you. Why? Because you've taught him to do what you say and you know what's best for him. There's a difference between naughtiness and obedience.

IS DISCIPLINE NECESSARY?

There's no point in asking, 'How do I discipline my child?' unless you're convinced that discipline is really necessary. I guess that the question about the necessity of discipline is coupled with another question, 'What does discipline actually accomplish?'

More than anything else, discipline convinces your children that you love them. You must stay a million miles away from the idea that discipline will crush your children. It will actually do the opposite. When God disciplines us, we know that He loves us. Because we want our children to be the most loved on planet earth, we discipline them. Then they know where they stand and are certain that we love them.

In their excellent book, *Raising Kids who Hunger for God*, Benny and Sheree Phillips say about discipline:

> *'It is one of our children's needs rather than simply a tactic for dealing with bad behaviour'.*

Raising Kids Who Hunger for God, Benny and Sheree Phillips, Chosen Books, a division of Baker Book House, Grand Rapids, Michigan, 1991.

Children actually need discipline. It's good for them, a security. You don't discipline your children primarily for your sake, but for theirs. That's why discipline is necessary.

The Victorians were very hot on discipline. Children then were seen and not heard. They'd sit round the table, and the rod would be right there in front of them. If they moved, they'd get it. But this discipline was often wrongly motivated. It wasn't for the children's sake at all. It was for the parents' sake. They wanted their children to reflect good Victorian standards rather than biblical standards that are always surrounded by love, understanding and a care for the good of the child — and not a fear of what other people will think about us as a family. We must discipline our children primarily for their sake, not ours.

From time to time you read articles about rebellious teenagers who despise their parents. These teenagers don't hate their parents because they disciplined them, but because they didn't. When they were children they needed discipline, but their parents were too weak to administer it. That's why they lost respect for their parents and questioned their love. That's why they rebelled.

So here I am, a parent confronted with a decision: 'Should I discipline my children or not?' The world screams it's modern ideas at me: 'Let them express themselves, do what they like' and that sort of thing. And I'm thinking, 'What do I do?' We're back to where we were before: Do we follow the philosophy of our age, or live by the Word of God?

Zig Ziglar, in his book, *Raising Positive Kids in a Negative World* says this about physical discipline:

'Question — is physical discipline necessary? Answer — yes. It is for several reasons, primarily children between the ages of about 2 and 12 live out a decade in life when they lack the maturity to listen to, understand, and responsibly follow their parents' instructions. Part of the fabric of humanity is a matter of individual will. Children come into the world, into the family and into society with little control over that will. One of the most significant aspects of maturity is learning to be self controlled or self disciplined. A young child simply will not have this kind of maturity. Discipline literally means to train and youngsters need a lot of training. Most of it should be of a verbal or spoken nature but some of it will have to be of a firm physical nature. As a rule of thumb, when your child is wilfully disobedient towards you that's when physical action is necessary. It could be the swiftest, surest way to get your message across.' Ibid.

When we discipline our children, we must understand that we're dealing with their wills. They aren't mature enough to be able to work things out properly. We're there to help them.

CHAPTER 10

What does discipline accomplish?

Let me give you some things that discipline will accomplish in your children's lives so you can see how vital it really is.

IT EXPRESSES LOVE
By now I hope you've got the message.

IT GIVES SECURITY
When children understand the boundaries and are kept within them, they feel secure. You must make sure that the boundaries don't change from day to day.

IT BRINGS PEACE INTO THE HOME
When you discipline your children, you'll bring a sense of order and peace into your home. I've had fathers say to me, 'My home is so chaotic' and I think, 'I know. I've been there.' They then wonder what I'm going to do about it. And I say, 'What are you going to do?' I told one father, 'You bring peace into your home'. He replied, 'It's not as simple as that'. And I said, 'Yes, it is. You're the father of that family. You

bring peace. Change things, make decisions, have breakfast earlier, get the children to bed on time. You bring peace into your home when you say, "This is my home. This is what's going to happen"'.

IT SHOWS WHO'S BOSS
Children need to know who's in charge. The issue of authority in the home is very simple: if parents don't exercise it, then their children will take it. There's no such thing as 'no authority' there. I've been in homes where two or three year-old children rule and reign. They make the decisions and their parents run all over the place trying to placate them and meet their wants.

IT SETS THE BOUNDARIES
Boundary setting is very important, but it can differ from family to family — which can lead to complications. Children will argue, 'But John's allowed to stay up until 9.30 p.m. So why can't I stay up too?' The answer is simple, 'Tough! While you're in this family this is how it is.'

IT BRINGS CONSISTENCY
Children need a sense of consistency throughout the day, the week, even their lives.

IT PREVENTS REBELLION
I don't think I need to elaborate on that. It prevents or checks rebellion.

IT BRINGS RESPECT
Discipline helps children to learn how to respect their parents and other adults too. If your children aren't disciplined they'll not only have no respect for you, they'll have no respect for anyone else either. When our children have had birthday

parties at home, they've always invited friends from non-christian families — which is great. The trouble is that they can't cope with me. I say, 'Now we'll play musical statues' and I get the response, 'But I don't want to.' My reply to that is, 'Well you're still going to play it.' And once the game has started, surprise, surprise — they love it! Discipline will bring respect for you and for others as well.

Here's another quote from Benny Phillips:

> *'Discipline — for most of us the word itself produces negative thoughts. Structure, boundaries, restrictions, spanking, lost privileges, perhaps even thoughts of harshness and anger will come to mind. Sheree and I have met few adults who were raised by parents who disciplined them lovingly and consistently. Some were punished by frustrated parents who, after trying various means of coercion, resorted to spanking in anger. For others corporal punishment was seldom used and they were allowed to get by with attitudes and behaviour they are now unwilling to tolerate in their own children. Tragically, others were slapped, pushed, shouted at or beaten. It's no wonder that child discipline is a difficult topic of consideration. In reaction to the ineffective or harsh means with which our generation was disciplined today's parents find themselves shrinking from this important aspect of parenting, fearing that we may duplicate the mistakes of their parents we muddle through hoping that our children will turn out okay. They will not. Why is it that children need discipline? to punish them for irritating behaviour? to teach them who is boss in the family? to convince them to do what they've been told? The humble parent will admit to the temptation of thinking*

*of these and other inappropriate reasons. Discipline is
an important factor in our children's lives.' Ibid.*

Here are the reasons why discipline is so important:
It helps expose children to their sin, natures, and thus their
need of a Saviour.
It leads them out of selfishness, foolishness and rebellion
and into conformity with Jesus Christ.
It helps to develop their character and enables them to interact
well with others.
The most important fruit of discipline is that it equips our
children to mature from the discipline that will eventually
come from God.

This is where you're going to clash with people. Your biblical
view of man affects why and how you discipline your
children. If you believe that children are born in sin, you'll
know why they behave badly and you'll recognise that you
as a parent have the responsibility to discipline them. Of
course, discipline won't bring them to salvation, but it will
point them in the right direction.

Now it's probably true to say that a lot of modern child
psychologists don't believe in God, or that man is created in
His image, or that he's separated from God by sin. So it's no
wonder that we aren't going to agree with them. We start a
million miles apart. You could say to them, 'Well, one of the
reasons why I discipline my children is because they're born
in sin and that sin needs to be dealt with.' They're not going
to sit back and say, 'Yes fine. What a good point. We must
consider that in our next seminar!' You're going to be in the
minority.

When you read modern secular psychology books about children, you must understand that you're approaching discipline from a totally different angle. You believe that your children are born in sin. Well, a secular psychologist might come along and say, 'You need to converse with them and let them openly express their inner turmoil.' But you know that if you allow that, sin will run riot. So you can't go along with this sort of advice. Because of that, the world is bound to have problems with you over the way you want to raise your children.

Yes, discipline is necessary. Your view of man, and therefore of your children, affects the way that you bring them up. You must choose whether you listen to the philosophy of modern secular psychologists or to the Word of God.

CHAPTER 11

Smacking

What does the Bible say about this subject? Here's where we all get hot under the collar We recall that we've said, 'Yes, Lord. I want to obey your Word' until we find out what the Word says! Well, here are four verses in Proverbs about it: 'He who spares the rod, hates his son, but he who loves him is careful to discipline him' (13:24). 'Folly (or sin) is bound up in the heart of a child, but the rod of discipline will drive it far from him' (22:15). 'Do not withhold discipline from a child; if you punish him with the rod, he will not die. Punish him with the rod and save his soul from death' (23:13,14). 'The rod of correction imparts wisdom, but a child left to himself disgraces his mother' (29:15).

Until about two decades ago this teaching formed the basis of all Judaeo-christian thinking throughout the western world. We knew that everyone before us had lived by the principles in Proverbs and the idea of physical discipline really wasn't a problem. Then suddenly we were 'enlightened' and had to start accepting something new. The question we need to ask is this: In the last twenty years are we better with our children than all those who have gone before us? You need only look around at society to know the answer to that.

Hebrews 12 suggests that children will need exactly the same discipline under the New Covenant as they did under the Old. The writer to the Hebrews speaks about fathers disciplining their children — presumably by smacking. Smacking isn't the only way we discipline our children, but it's the major one. If you tell someone, 'We smack our children' they'll immediately think, 'child abuse'. They're visualising an out of control parent landing blows on the children, who haven't a clue what's going on. But this couldn't be further from the truth. This is not the smacking we advocate, as we'll see later.

Child abuse has become a genuine issue, no one would deny that. There's an organisation called STOP which is very determined about the issue of child punishment. And in four European nations it's against the law to smack your child — whether it's with a wooden spoon or your hands. People have been fined for smacking their children and there's even a suggestion that they'll go to prison for it, or have their children taken away.

That's the way modern thinking has gone and our so-called free society is now imposing restrictions on us, telling us how we should raise our children. This has obviously led to a great deal of concern and confusion over the subject of smacking your own child. Which is more important? Obeying the law of the land which militates against the Word of God, or obeying the Word of God for the sake of our children? We mustn't back off because we fear what people will think of us. That would be doing things for our sake when we should be working in the interests of our children.

The Bible doesn't teach us to swipe out at our children. When I'm in the supermarket or the street I sometimes see a child playing around. Then his mother comes up. She doesn't say anything but just hits him. Most people object to that and I think it's totally out of order. Christians believe in loving correction in a loving, ordered environment. Of course, physical punishment will always be dangerous because it could easily go wrong. But we don't throw the baby out with the bath water just because some people have made mistakes. Never discipline a child when you are angry. If you are constantly losing your temper, then talk it through with someone and ask the Holy Spirit to help you, so that you can go on to obey God's Word.

There's a problem with this issue of smacking. Society questions whether or not we should do it, but people seem to ignore this instruction. In a survey in this country, 89 per cent of parents admitted to smacking their children. Most of them do it out of frustration or anger, and a high percentage of that 89 per cent feel terribly guilty about it because it's done mostly out of anger. That's tragic. You should be able to say, 'Yes we smack our children, but we don't feel the slightest bit guilty. That's because we never do it out of frustration or anger, but because we love our children. We're proud of the fact that we discipline them because we know it's right and it produces the correct results'.

I'll just touch on a couple of things before I get down to the nitty gritty. First, make sure that you deal with any negative attitudes or memories that you may have about your childhood experiences of home. A lot of people say, 'My parents brought me up this way, so I'm not going to do this or that'. You may have had too much discipline or too little, but you mustn't base what you do now on your past experience. As a married couple, or a single parent, you must come to the Word of God and start again. You need to say, 'Lord, please show us how we should discipline our children'. You must deal with negative memories that may be there.

Then you must make sure that the Bible is your ultimate authority. I'm staggered at the number of conversations I have with christian couples who totally refute any kind of punishment or discipline of their children. 'We know it's in the Bible,' they say, 'but that's not the way we do it now. We're modernised. We've come to some sort of maturity.' People who think this have a problem with the Word of God. They must either throw out the biblical teaching on discipline, or embrace it as teaching that works, that produces results, that sets people free.

The experts are always changing their minds on how to raise children. When Liz went into hospital to have our first child, she was told, 'This is the latest thing we've found about new-born babies'. Two years later Liz had baby number two and she was informed, 'Oh, we don't believe that any more. What we now think is this'. Two more years passed and we were having our third baby. By then, the nurses had scrapped what they had said and were back to where they were six years before. It's incredible! The poor mums are totally confused. They want to be left alone to raise their children. And they think they know what they're doing.

It's a contradiction. The experts are always changing their minds on child raising. But when every other system has failed, God's Word will stand for ever. If it offends today, it will offend the next generation and the next. His Word will never change. It will always be there — available for us to read and live by.

CHAPTER 12

How
to
smack

When I first heard someone speak about using the rod I didn't have any children of my own and I was in confusion. I didn't like what was being said. I wasn't raised this way and I became easily offended and reacted emotionally.

It's a different issue — hearing something when you haven't got children, and hearing when you have. Here I am, four children later, an advocate of the principles that I had heard — because I gulped hard, disciplined my first child and found that discipline worked.

The Bible says we should use the rod. In today's terminology the rod could be a wooden kitchen spoon or something like that. Why should we use a 'rod'? Here are some reasons:
1. It's biblical.
2. It works. Thousands of Mums and Dads throughout the world will testify to this.
3. It's a neutral object. Your children will see a wooden spoon as something apart from you. Hands are used for things like

hugging and expressing love. Sometimes I see a little child wince or duck when his Mum moves her hand to scratch her head. That's really sad. He sees the hand as something that might lash out at him. Liz and I have found that smacking our children with our hands has proved to be woefully inadequate.

4. It prevents the parent from reacting in anger. By the time you reach the kitchen drawer to get the spoon, you've counted from one to ten and have collected yourself. I never lash out at my children suddenly. I explain, 'Right, you've broken the rules and I'm going to discipline you now.' Then I get the spoon and administer the discipline. This is a very helpful common sense thing.

5. You put the 'rod' away after you've used it. This reinforces to the child that the incident which prompted the discipline is now over.

Our children have always been disciplined like this, and they've never had a problem with it. In fact we laugh and joke about it together.

Where do we hit the child? Well, to quote Larry Tomczak, 'All children come equipped with a bottom'. That seems to be the perfect place to exercise discipline. How many times do we smack a child? Once. Some people won't agree with this, but I feel that if you're going to smack more than once, your anger may rise up again. I've found that one hit is sufficient to discipline a child.

Lots of parents ask us if the wooden spoon treatment hurts. I say, 'Try it out on yourself and you'll know that it does!' That's the whole object of the exercise. It's got to hurt because that's what deters the child. He knows that when he does something wrong, he's going to suffer the consequences. So he decides that maybe it's not worth sinning in the first place. If you don't hurt your children when you discipline them, they'll laugh at you and the discipline will be meaningless. You'll lose your authority and the sense of direction in the situation. We've found that smacking a child works and is absolutely essential.

There are lots of desperate parents around. They're being deprived of the answer to the question, 'How do I raise my children?' They've got small children and don't know what to do with them. They're at their wits' end and are turning to dreadful alternatives. Let's look at some of them.

DON'T REASON OR BARGAIN WITH YOUR CHILD

'If you do that again you're not going to have any sweets tomorrow.' This doesn't make the slightest bit of difference to that child because he knows he's going to get the sweets anyway. Most parents who coax and reason with their children eventually give in anyway. This sort of bargaining also gives the child the opportunity to come back to you on an issue. You've given them the room to say, 'My will is as important at yours' when you should have settled the matter by swift discipline.

DON'T SEND YOUR CHILD TO HIS/HER ROOM

I was always sent to my bedroom and it was there that I learnt to rebel more than anywhere else. I discovered new swear words and built up my aggression. Sending a child to his bedroom doesn't deal with the issue that needs to be confronted. Parents, particularly with pre-senior school children, must confront them immediately they've done wrong. If you tell them, 'You've done this, these are the consequences and you'll have to go without that' then you're putting off the issue. You're leaving a time gap so that you can't deal with the matter immediately. I'm against that.

DON'T SHOUT LOUDLY

If your children know you're in control, you can raise them in a disciplined way without ever having to raise your voice.

CHAPTER 13

An emotive subject

I once watched a television chat show about raising a family. Most of it was absolutely terrible. One woman on the programme said that she regularly smacked her children. Another couple said that they smacked their son once but felt so terrible about it that they decided never to do this again. The problem was that a year later this child was taking eggs out of the fridge and smashing them on the floor. The parents refused to smack him, so he kept throwing the eggs around.

They had an American child psychologist there and the debate began. The mother who disciplined her children was a wonderful lady. She told the couple, 'Give me your child and in three months' time you'll have no problems at all'. The couple said, 'Oh we can't possible discipline our children because it's so hurtful. We had so many inner hurts in our childhood and it was terrible hearing him cry out when we hit him.' The interviewer was obviously on their side.

The mother had all her children playing happily around her. At one point the interviewer asked her children what they thought about discipline. They had no problem with it at all. He then turned to the child psychologist and asked, 'If we aren't allowed to smack our children, how do we stop a child who smashes eggs?' The psychologist said that he must be disturbed and should go through some psychological and psychiatric counselling. This deeply offended and angered his mother and father who wouldn't believe that their son needed this kind of help simply because he was breaking eggs. When the programme finished, it was clear that the only answer was to discipline the child.

I mention this programme to challenge you. If you've got a better alternative than the Word of God, you'd better tell people about it quickly. I can't think of any viable alternative to the way that the Bible tells us to raise our children.

Contrary to most secular opinion, when parents smack their children in a loving environment they don't produce insecure children who fear their wrath. Rather, discipline produces happy and obedient children. The clearly defined standards give them a strong sense of security. They understand the love of God the Father and have a strong sense of self worth. In the final analysis you've got to look at the fruit. Then you can see what really works.

I was speaking at a conference and at the end of one meeting I was publicly harassed by a woman who vehemently disagreed with my teaching about discipline and the Word of God. She went on and on while I tried to be polite and calm her down. Afterwards, the pastor of the church she attended came to me and said, 'I just thought I'd let you know that her children are the worst behaved in the church'. I said, 'Why didn't you stand up and say that publicly?' Obviously he couldn't have done that, but it would have helped my cause!

The way people raise their children is a very emotive subject. People react — as this woman did. But in the end it's the fruit that proves whether discipline works or not. As I've said, my children have no problem with discipline. It's part of life, something that's even fun. If a rule against smacking children is ever brought into our nation, my children will readily tell their teacher that they're disciplined in this way. That's because they don't understand the fuss. In fact when they discovered that some children in their class never got disciplined by their parents they said things like, 'Dad, it's terrible! Chloe never ever gets smacked for anything. She'll be naughty, and undisciplined'. I think my children should be writing this book instead of me!

When Liz and I give seminars on discipline, we get many questions. Some of the questioners say, 'I've tried smacking but it doesn't work'. I reply, 'It's not that smacking doesn't work. It's that you're doing it wrong'. In the next chapter I'll go through the process of how to discipline your child because I actually think this is the key.

CHAPTER 14

When do we start disciplining?

There are two stages. Stage one begins when the baby starts to move and understands the word, 'No' — and babies understand far more than they can articulate. If you're a real cool baby you'll not learn to speak for ages!

A baby understands that inflection of your voice from a very, very young age. From the moment that baby moves, reaches out, touches the Hi-fi with its finger knowing that it's not allowed to, that's the moment disciplines starts.

It starts with a dab on the hand when your baby is eight or nine months old. The response when you do that for the first time is interesting. 'No' you're saying. 'You're not allowed to touch the Hi-fi in our front room' — dab. The little baby looks around at you, mortified, and you know that a process has started. You walk out of the room and he crawls around and touches the Hi-fi button and then pulls a pile of magazines onto the floor. You race around after him, saying, 'Stop it!' (dab). You almost need to go to aerobics just to be fit enough to raise children! It's exhausting and exasperating, and you begin to realise that this may be alright for a while, but is woefully inadequate in the long run.

When this child is twelve to eighteen months old you move into the second stage — proper discipline — which is rather more effective than the hand dabbing. I'll tell you what Liz and I found helpful here.

First, the child has been caught in the act. That's important, because you should never swipe out at a child when he doesn't understand that what he's done is wrong. So we set the rules and then warn our children once and once only. Some parents give repeated warnings. 'If you do that, I'm going to ...' they say. Then five minutes later they say it again. What the child thinks is, 'I can just milk this as long as I like'. So you warn them, 'If you throw food across the table, you'll be disciplined'. When the child jettisons his bun over the table, there's no more debate or coaxing. He knows the rules and that he's deliberately disobeyed them. He's been caught in the act and expects to be punished.

When our child is caught in the act, he must repent, then we'll forgive him and put the matter behind us. That's exactly the way God disciplines us. We know we've broken the rules and repent. He forgives us and puts our sin out of His mind. And we walk away as if the issue has never happened.

Second, we take the child away from the scene of the crime. We never discipline our children before other members of the family or in a crowd. We find somewhere to take them, and while we're taking them there, we've got time to work out what we're going to do and how we're going to do it. If we're at home, we'll go into the kitchen.

At this point you'll get different reactions because all children are different. Some will say, 'OK, let's go into the kitchen' with a 'See if I care' attitude. While for others the very idea of going into the kitchen causes the tears to flow. These are both brilliant ways of avoiding the issue. Tearfulness and heart rending wails can tempt you to say, 'Well, never mind, dear. We won't punish you this time.' But having said what you're going to do, you must carry it through. It's also good for you because it calms you down.

Once we arrive in the kitchen I explain the situation to my child. Some parents miss out this important step. I say, 'You know why you're going to get disciplined. It's because I told you not to do this and you've disobeyed me. In this house, if you disobey, you get the wooden spoon. Is that clear?'

While I'm talking, they might be crying and fretting. A lot of parents have problems with this. They plough on while their child is having a tantrum and then smack him while they are all in a state. No, first you get their attention. For example, Julia will be crying and I'll say, 'Julia, look at me.' At this point she'll do anything but look at me. She'll gaze down or around — and most children will do the same. I'll continue, 'Come on, Julia, look at me.' Then when I've got her attention I'll say, 'You've disobeyed me, haven't you?' I'm speaking truth, making sure she understands the issue and why she's being punished. It isn't a fight. I'm bigger than she is. This sort of discipline is difficult when your children are fourteen or fifteen and you're looking up at them! But if you work at it when they're young, you won't have to worry when they're older because the principles will have been built in.

I'll then get hold of Julia and lean her towards me. If your child is in nappies, they'll have to come down and the process will take time. I'll give one whack on the bottom with the spoon and nine times out of ten they'll cry because it hurts. I'll wait while they're crying, then I'll get eye contact again and say, 'Now calm down'. Next, I'll ask, 'Now what do you say?' Often there'll be a very quiet indistinct 'Sorry'. To that, I'll say, 'Julia, I didn't quite hear what that was'. This is an important part of the process — it's repentance. I continue, 'So what do you say? Now speak clearly.' 'Sorry.' 'Sorry who?' 'Sorry, Daddy (or Mummy).' 'OK, Daddy forgives you. I love you and you know that's why I disciplined you.'

Then comes the greatest part of the whole process and my children will cope with smacks because they know what comes afterwards. It's now that I hug them and affirm, 'I forgive you'. You must never discipline a child without hugging.

This process is a million miles away from angrily swiping out at a child in a supermarket and then leaving him to wipe away the tears. We're punishing, the child is repenting, we're forgiving and then making sure that he knows he's forgiven and secure in our love. I may even say, 'Now you know why Daddy smacked you?' 'Yes.' 'You won't do it again, will you?' 'No.'

Sometimes I'll have to instruct them about what happens in the future. If their conduct has involved another child, they may have to resolve this with that person. I've said to Daniel, 'Now, Daniel, I've forgiven you but you must go to Lucy and hug her'. I'll follow him and watch him obey me half-heartedly. Then I'll say, 'Now come on. I want you to really embrace'. He's learning how the process works. And when he's hugged his sister properly, he knows that the issue has been dealt with. The wooden spoon is put away and he walks out of the kitchen totally forgiven. He also understands that if he disobeys again the whole process will be repeated.

Maybe you're thinking, 'This all sounds so time consuming' and I agree — it is. Sometimes you will come home from work exhausted and one of the children misbehaves. You know what you're supposed to do, but you're tired. It's then that you'll have to force myself to get up and sort things out.

All of our children have been regularly disciplined, although some of them have needed far more discipline than others, according to their personalities. They're different, but the principles are the same and the process will be repeated again and again. It's likely that when your children are between the ages of two and six or seven, you'll spend more time in the kitchen than you will outside it! The discipline will seem endless. But remember, it's worth it. It's worth all the effort and aggro. You just keep going because you're building a principle. When your children reach the age of seven, eight or nine, you'll be disciplining them less and less because they understand the principle. Discipline them early and you'll reap the reward later.

Some christian books say that smacking is the last resort. They tell you to do this and that, and then if you really can't think of anything else to do, smack your child. I refute that. Smacking isn't a last resort. It's a clear part of the parcel of raising our children.

Now sometimes there's a reason why your children are irritable. Perhaps they were up late the previous night and are really tired. You need to discern that, because there's no point your disciplining your child if he's tired or ill. On the other hand, you mustn't use tiredness as an excuse. Some parents are always excusing their children, 'Sorry about Sarah but she's tired' they say. Is she always tired? Wouldn't putting her to bed earlier help? Is this a genuine reason or an excuse?

Finally, discipline must be consistent. When parents say, 'Smacking doesn't work' the reason is likely to be that they're inconsistent in their application of this discipline. If you forget everything else I've said, remember the word consistency, because this will be a major key to your fruitfulness in raising your children. If you're inconsistent, you'll blow your cover. You'll be inconsistent if one child gets away with something when the other child doesn't, or if the child gets away with something one day but not the next. Discipline must be regular and consistent.

Grandparents can be troublesome when it comes to discipline. Have you ever noticed what happens after your children have visited their grandparents? They come home wanting this and that, sweets, treats — you name it. The reason is that their grandparents have been giving them these things and they want the process to continue. There's an inconsistency creeping in and the children are in danger of getting away with blue murder.

At first, my parents, who are christians, objected to the way we disciplined our children. I told them that we were clear about how we were going to do it, and they reluctantly let us get on with it. As the years went by they saw how other children were brought up. Then they came to us and said, 'We just want you to know that we were wrong. We've seen the way you've raised our grandchildren and we're thrilled with the results.' It's so important to be consistent. The standards mustn't change regardless of whether the children are with others or with you.

CHAPTER 15

What do we discipline?

S ome parents wonder what to discipline in their children. I think that there are three categories:

1. OBVIOUS REBELLION

You must deal with obvious rebellion — there's no debate about it. If you tell your child not to touch something and he deliberately disobeys you, he's challenged your authority and you're immediately into the discipline process. If you change your mind or back off, then you pull the rug from under your feet and give your child the permission to challenge whatever you say. You must carry the discipline through straight away.

2. BAD ATTITUDES

If you're the pastor of a church and there's obvious rebellion against the Word of God, then people expect you to exercise discipline. What they perhaps don't realise is that most of the pastoral ministry is about dealing not with rebellion, but with attitudes — complaining, grumbling, back biting, negativism, not going along with what's been said and all that sort of thing.

I think it's the same when we come to the subject of raising our children. Most of us have no problem disciplining clear rebellion, but don't see that we need to deal with attitudes which aren't so obvious. It always amazes me when people say, 'I'm staggered that you discipline your children over sulkiness' (or some other attitude). I think that this is one of the first things you discipline a child for.

When Daniel was one to two years old, Liz and I started to notice that when we told him off he would vanish. One day we found him lying in the hall with his head in his hands and his lips turned up. He was actually avoiding confrontation by going into a sulk. In fact he often behaved in a very sulky way. Then we suddenly thought that if we didn't train him out of his sulkiness, he'd be unbearable by the time he got to his teens. So we sat down with him and said, 'Now look, every time we tell you off you sulk and turn your lip up. You avoid us and refuse to look at us. Well I'm going to discipline you every time this happens.' So the discipline process began. He understood what we were doing and it was wonderful to see the change that began to take place in his life.

Answering back is another bad attitude. That starts when your child is from eight to ten years old. Emily was a great one for answering back. We told her, 'Whenever we confront you, you always say something like, "Why should I?" or "Do I have to?" or "I don't want to"'. And she replied, 'No, I don't!' That's an attitude that needs to be disciplined.

Maybe you think that this is getting a bit over the top, but we don't see it that way. If a child hits another child over the head with a toy car, there's no doubt that he needs discipline. But it's just as crucial to apply the same discipline to things like grumbling, complaining and disrespect. So let us encourage you to broaden your scope about what needs to be disciplined. You don't want to find yourself dealing with the obvious while your child is getting away with an awful lot of other things that you don't notice.

3. HOUSE RULES

Other people will have different standards from you. Once you've set your particular boundaries, you must ensure that you keep to them. When there's rebellion or a wrong attitude, you must deal with it and not be like some couples who let their children get away with blue murder. I'll give you two examples of this.

I was at a church weekend away. At meal times I sat at a table with a couple and their young son. This child ate only what he wanted to eat and had probably done this since he was about two or three. His parents were very embarrassed because he wouldn't eat anything that he was given. On the Sunday the boy's Dad said to me, 'You may have noticed that our child doesn't like to eat what he's given.' I replied, 'Funnily enough, yes I have.' Then he said, 'It's sad, isn't it?' 'No' I answered. 'It isn't sad. Who's decided what he does and doesn't like?' 'Well' he said, 'we've just allowed him to decide for himself'.

I'm amazed at this. If you let a child decide for himself what he wants to eat, he'll end up liking only beefburgers, chips and tomato sauce. Then you won't be able to do anything about it or take him anywhere without being embarrassed by his eating habits.

I said to them, 'I think it's a matter of discipline. My children don't like certain types of food, but we put some of it on their plates and they have to eat it because we're training them to be grateful and to do what they're told. If you take your son and discipline him like this, he'll begin to eat other things.'

Two or three weeks later I had a letter from this couple. 'It's amazing!' they said. 'We gave our son food that he wouldn't eat and we disciplined him. He still refused it, so we disciplined him again. Then he started to eat it. This little breakthrough has transformed our lives.' It's not just up to our children to decide these things for themselves. We must be involved.

This brings me onto my second illustration. Parents sometimes say to me, 'We have a real problem with our child. He just won't go to bed when we tell him. And if we put him to bed he won't stay there.' I just think to myself, 'Who decides who goes to bed and when?' And I tell them, 'You work out when he goes to bed, and if he doesn't want to go, you make him go.'

You may decide that your child needs to go to bed at ten o'clock. Or you may think that seven o'clock is better. Whatever you resolve to do, go for it. I may think you're very unwise to allow your three year-old to go to bed later than six o'clock. But that's up to you. If you can't get any time on your own in the evenings because your little child is up with you until eight or nine o'clock, that's not his fault, it's yours. If he won't stay in bed, you discipline him to stay. You decide what you want to happen and then act on what you've decided.

SINGLE PARENTS
At this point I just want to say something about single parents. I've already quoted the verse: 'God sets the lonely in families'

(Ps. 68:6) and it's clear that single parents are included in His family. Obviously, God's intention is for a child to be brought up by his mother and father, but that's not always possible. Where there are single parents in the church, the members need to see their responsibility as the family of God to support and help them to raise their children. Some of our church members have particularly reached out to single mothers. They provide encouragement, support and advice wherever they can. Single parents are as much a part of the church family as anyone else.

So if you're a single parent, please don't despair or try to work it all out on your own. Stick with it. Ask people for help and accept their advice. If they can't give it, find someone who can. Get involved with others as much as you can. All the principles mentioned here work for you too.

CHAPTER 16

Liz answers some questions

Before I go on to some of the questions that people ask us about raising children, I just want to encourage you that it's worth investing your lives in your children. You may think it's years of hard work, but there's such fulfilment as you see your children grow up. Sometimes you'll feel weary and you won't be able to see much fruit — especially when the children are going through a difficult time. Let me encourage you not to give up but to be confident in what God has given you. Keep at it and you'll start to see the fruit.

Emily's in her teens now and she's got a great character and a real maturity. God has helped us to train and discipline her and now we're seeing the fruit of what we've been doing. Many of her friends at school come from very difficult backgrounds. They know that she's a christian and that she comes from a secure background, so they go to her for advice. When she gets home, she tells me about the sort of things that are worrying them and I'm amazed that God is using her to help them. But it's really all part of the fruit of what we've been putting in to her.

Now let's get on to some of the questions that people ask us about raising children. Some of these areas have already been mentioned in other chapters — but we mention them again to emphasise their importance.

WHAT ABOUT GRANDPARENTS?

David's already touched on this, but I'd like to emphasise again what he said. I feel it's really important for couples to decide together how they're going to raise their children and then to sit down with their parents and chat things through.

When our children are going to visit their grandparents, or even to a friend's house, I sit down and talk to them. I remind them of how we've brought them up and what we expect of them. They listen to me and know exactly how we want them to behave. The lines of communication are open and they're clear about where we stand. This is really important.

WHAT ABOUT NEGATIVE RESPONSES?

Children will have bad attitudes. They'll whine, cry and try to get out of things. They'll be out playing in the street, you'll call them in and will be bombarded with negative attitudes. Another simple request will be met with equal resistance. You say, 'Please clear the table now'. Then suddenly you'll find yourself reasoning with your child about why you're asking him to clear the table now. Stop and question, 'Why do I have to give ten reasons for this action?' Surely you're just trying to teach your child how to be helpful. There may be a time when you can sit him down and explain why you expect him to do chores around the house. But when you give him a simple direction, you're expecting him to respond with simple obedience.

Immediately children start to whine or cry, you've got to deal with it. Some children seem to go through a phase when they're unwilling to obey simple commands. Instead, they seem to contest everything you say. You'll think to yourself, 'Only a month ago they were willing to do almost anything. What's happened now?' You must be aware of this phase and home in on it. You need to instruct them carefully and specifically to stop them moaning. If they continue to do it, you'll have to smack them and explain how you expect them to behave. They won't like this, but it's all part of the training. You must work hard and persevere.

The breakthrough will come. Their behaviour will begin to improve. Instead of whinging and moaning, they'll become willing to help you. Then it's really important to praise and encourage them. Often the best time to do this is at night when it's quiet. Maybe they've had a bath and they're lying in bed, relaxed and sleepy. That's the time when you can have some wonderful conversations with them.

Sometimes I sit on the side of the bed with them. I stroke their heads and talk the whole thing through. I explain why I had to discipline them for moaning and they really understand. Then I say that I've noticed the change in their behaviour. Maybe I'll mention certain times when they willingly got up and cleared the table or tidied their bedroom. I'll tell them, 'You're much more co-operative and willing. I'm proud of you.' It's so important that you follow discipline with praise and encouragement.

WHAT ABOUT TANTRUMS?

Some children are far more volatile and impulsive than others. They quickly get in a temper about things and just let themselves go. They lash out with their arms and legs and look as though they're going into a fit. We must recognise these signs and nip them in the bud. They often begin when the child is very small.

You'll probably know when they're on the verge of a temper tantrum. They're engrossed in something or don't want to leave the beach. Then you see their little legs start to wobble and you say, 'Now you stop those legs wobbling and let's talk about this'. Of course, you'll need to exercise common sense and be reasonable, but if they refuse to do what you say, you'll have to discipline them. You can't have a discussion with a child who is starting to let it all go.

WHAT ABOUT DISCIPLINING MORE THAN ONCE?

Maybe you give your child a reasonable request, 'Please put away your toys now'. If he refuses to do this, you must discipline him. If, after discipline, he still refuses to obey you, he needs further discipline. In other words, you take him through the whole discipline process again and you send him back to fulfil your original request.

This won't happen very often. In my experience with four children, you could probably count the number of times on one hand. But you must be consistent and deal with disobedience. Your children need to know that you're in control and that they can't win. It's also important that you don't lose your temper. You must remain calm and make it clear that you're expecting them to do as you've asked.

WHAT ABOUT DISCIPLINING IN PUBLIC?

We want to trust our children to be well-behaved, sensible and mature wherever they are — whether they're at home or in a public place. To achieve this goal, we must begin when our children are very young — maybe two or three years old — because it's then that they'll test the limits of what we expect of them.

So you may be out shopping in a supermarket and they start misbehaving. They want to get out of the buggy or the trolley and run around the shop. You know that this is dangerous and that your request 'Stay in the buggy' is perfectly reasonable. But they don't think so. Discipline under these circumstances is time consuming. You've got to leave the trolley, find somewhere to take them — like a toilet — and show them that you're not accepting this sort of behaviour.

When they were younger, our children seemed to go through seasons of this kind of rebellion and at those times I actually took my wooden spoon to the shops with me just in case they didn't conform to my expectations. I'd encourage you to carry through with this kind of discipline when you're out, otherwise, when they're older, you won't be able to trust them in public places.

Dave and I can now take all four of our children out to a restaurant and relax with them. When we went on holiday to America, we took our children out for a meal and the waitresses were stunned that they sat still for the whole time. So many parents have problems in this area. They haven't consistently disciplined their children and now they can't stop them doing whatever they like wherever they are. Naturally, you've got to use your common sense, but you must deal with open rebellion. The answer isn't to placate them by buying them sweets every time you go shopping. That's a trap you'll find it hard to get out of. You must discipline them and later you'll see the fruit of that.

WHAT ABOUT OTHER PEOPLE DISCIPLINING YOUR CHILDREN?

I always like to leave my children with people I can trust, people who share the same kind of values. They may be babysitters or friends who are visiting for the day. Whether you allow them to discipline your children is up to you. And if you're the babysitter, you can't discipline other people's children unless you've got the parents' permission. If the children of non-christian friends come round to your home, you must lay down the guidelines but you can't discipline those children as much as you might like.

WHAT ABOUT SIBLING FIGHTS?

You can discipline a child for rebellion against you, but what happens if more than one child is involved in the offence? You want peace and order in your home, but your children will fight one another. Often you can just let them get on with it and see how them manage. They can have a rough and tumble and sort themselves out. But when it comes to spitefulness, constant bickering, teasing and being really unkind they will need correction and possible discipline.

Suppose you weren't there when the offence took place. Sally says that John pushed her off the bed and John says that Sally hit him in the face. What do you do then? Well, you discuss it with them and then use your wisdom and judgement to decide who was to blame. Sometimes I've had to discipline both of them. I take the youngest first, then I come back and discipline the older one. It takes a long time. Then I get them together, tell them to look at each other and say, 'Right, now love and forgive each other'. After that they can resume their game and enjoy playing together.

If you start doing this, you'll have peace and order in your home. It takes a lot of effort and involvement, but you know that you're not just teaching them to handle each other, you're teaching them to handle things when they're in the world. In the school playground they see things that are unfair. They know the standards that they have been brought up by and when they're confronted by injustice, they'll learn to handle things with maturity.

When you're trying to work out who did what, be careful that you don't show favouritism. Some children are more strong willed and stroppy than others, some more easily fly off the handle. You must take these things into account and be fair and reasonable in your judgement. If you've got a large family, the younger children may tend to get away with things and the older ones might cover up for them. As the youngest of four, I used to get away with a lot because I was crafty and used to blame the others. So you must make sure that your judgement is impartial and not let any of them escape punishment for unacceptable behaviour.

These are just some of the many questions that are asked concerning loving discipline of our children. Every child is unique in his character and requires individual love and understanding. Every difficult situation that arises in their lives requires your involvement to bring direction and sometimes discipline.

The challenge to us is: Are we willing to be totally committed to training them and being a godly influence over their lives, or are we happy to let things drift and only now and again to get involved?

PART 3

Home sweet home:

is it always?

CHAPTER 17

The right environment

So far we've seen that children are a great joy to us when they're well trained. We've noted that discipline is vitally important in the raising of children. Now I want to look at the atmosphere that we create in our home for them.

I don't know much about plants, but I'm aware that if you want to grow a seed, it needs the right environment to flourish. This principle is exactly the same with children. The Bible describes children as plants (Ps. 144:12) and God wants us not just to train and discipline them, but also to create the right environment so that they will become mature.

The home is the place of influence for children. It's the place of love, care, peace and order. The school should not be left to provide these things, nor should the church. It's the responsibility of parents. It's your home and you are the number one person to raise your children.

It isn't always possible to create the ideal circumstances. However, there is an ideal and that's a good marriage. You can take on board all the right principles and yet discover that they're not working. And deep down you know why. It's because your relationship with your husband or wife isn't what it should be.

A good marriage is essential for the raising of children because everything flows from your marriage. You can pretend as much as you like, but the children will sense when things aren't right between Mum and Dad. So if you want to raise children in the right environment, you won't just concentrate on training and disciplining your children, you'll work hard at your marriage.

You can have a wonderful worldwide ministry. People can go to your meetings and think, 'This is amazing! What a tremendous dynamic ministry!' But if your marriage isn't right the whole thing will crumble in the end. A good marriage brings harmony into a home. It's essential because raising children is a partnership, a joint affair.

Liz and I are forever discussing our family life. We sit down at the kitchen table when the children aren't around and we talk about the way we're raising them. We know that much of it is to do with our relationship with one another. If that's not right, then our children are affected. But if our marriage is good and improving all the time, then out of that will flow the environment in which our children will thrive.

It's important that your children see you living harmoniously together and expressing love to one another. They need to see Mum and Dad caring for each other, kissing and cuddling. Have you noticed that when you get close together, they all want to plunge in and help the situation?

One of our children, Lucy, had the habit of saying things that weren't quite true. When Liz and I went to South Africa for two or three weeks, we left all the children behind and she was staying with a couple. One day she saw them kissing and cuddling in the kitchen and declared, 'My Mummy and Daddy never do that!' It didn't exactly help us to convince the couple that we had a really good marriage!

In a good marriage, a couple talks about lifestyle, diary and how much time they're spending with their children. Child raising isn't solely the responsibility of the mother. It's a joint responsibility. So Liz and I talk about how I can be more involved as the father of my children. We discuss each child's needs and how we're responding to them.

So a good environment begins with a good foundation which stems from a good marriage. If you neglect your marriage, you'll be in big problems. Let me encourage you to work hard at your relationship as husband and wife. Your harmony will bring harmony to your home.

BEING A SINGLE PARENT

If you are a single parent then the issue of a good environment applies to you as well — as do all the principles in this book. We meet many single parents who have adopted an almost defeatist attitude towards raising their children with the thinnest of hopes that if they work hard enough then their children might just about turn out okay. Of course, having a father and mother actively involved in raising children is the ideal, but if you find yourself alone, for whatever reason, then you must take a positive approach. It will be tough, but God's Word is for you too, and with His promises concerning your children you can raise your children with genuine confidence.

'A father to the fatherless, a defender of widows, is God in his holy dwelling. God sets the lonely in families' (Ps. 68:5,6) — that sounds like a good environment. If your children don't have a father — never forget that they have a wonderful heavenly Father. You may not have a 'completed family' but if God places the lonely in families then we do have the family of God.

Never feel that you are alone when it comes to raising your children as a single parent — God will provide you with families to assist you. We've seen several single parents helped wonderfully by other families coming alongside them or sometimes home groups can take some of the pressure off. God's people can never (and should never) replace you, but they can support and pray for you, and even take some of the strain.

More and more people are becoming single parents and the church needs to rise to the challenge before them. Single parents need even more encouragement and they certainly can't afford to be left to struggle alone. Find a good environment among God's people and your children will flourish.

CHAPTER 18

David talks about the role of the father

A right environment has to do with right roles. Here I'll be dealing with the role of the father and in the next chapter, Liz will cover the role of the mother. So let me ask, 'Where are the fathers?'

I once read a national newspaper article which questioned whether or not there would be any valid role for the so-called father in future generations. The article stated that the trend towards cohabitation instead of marriage gives greater freedom to each partner to come and go. It said that few men seriously consider fatherhood as part of the package. If the relationship breaks down after children are born, it's invariably the mother who feels responsible for them while the father just drifts away. You eventually end up with a potentially fatherless generation.

The father in marriage has become a somewhat distant and confused figure. Often he's not around and instead of investing his life in his family during his leisure time, he prefers to pursue his own activities. Many fathers don't understand their job description, let alone feel able to fulfil it. How many adults, when asked to reminisce about their own childhood, find it hard to remember the role that their father played? He was either not around very much, or was just there.

Television programmes don't help us. The father of the family is so often portrayed as incompetent, indecisive, irrelevant, an object of ridicule, certainly no one to model your life on. If you think I'm exaggerating just watch the next comedy series. We live in a society where family role models are being challenged and redefined. Few people now give positive instructions to fathers on how exactly they should play their part.

In the Bible God reveals Himself as our heavenly Father. He created families where His Fatherly nature would be reflected through earthly fathers — ordinary needy men like you and me. Without His earthly reflection, many children will grow up struggling to identify with a God who is their heavenly Father. So fathers have a tremendous responsibility and there are enormous consequences if we neglect it.

God never wanted the father's role to be taken over by the mother. Sadly, this is often the case — not by choice, but out of necessity. When people moan about, 'My overbearing mother,' I sometimes wonder if they've ever questioned the role of their father. It seems that fathers will often happily leave everything — especially the raising of the children — to the mother. 'That's her job,' they say. 'She's better than me anyway.' This is called neglecting your responsibility.

I've noticed that fathers often leave most of the training and discipline to the mother. They make excuses like, 'I'm too tired' and opt out. The poor mother has to look after her little children all day long and by evening she's at screaming point and hardly knows what to do. Dad comes home from a busy day at work and Mum says, 'These children are unbearable! I can't cope much longer.' Dad then picks up one of them and says, 'He's lovely. What are you talking about? What's the problem?' Rather than take up their responsibility in the family, fathers can try to make light of what's been happening at home. 'Don't be so stupid,' they say to their wives. 'The children aren't that bad.' What they're really doing is excusing themselves from dealing with an issue that is very real indeed.

There's a desperate need to restore fatherhood to our society today. We must have fathers who understand their role clearly, take it seriously and give themselves 100 per cent to their children. Fathers, you must hear this because it's important. It isn't primarily the responsibility of the mother to show affection, bring loving discipline, communicate by eye contact, set boundaries, train and instruct, plan fun times, bring security and make final decisions. These things are mainly the responsibility of the father.

My four children need me. I'm the only father they've got. Like me, you're probably very busy at work and may even travel away from home. It's when you begin to juggle your time and priorities that you're likely to slip into danger. What are your priorities? How high does your responsibility as a father come on your list? If you take your role as a father seriously, then you may have to sacrifice other things like money, career, prospects, and promotion. Your children consider you more important than what you do for a living.

There's a great family film about a dog called *Beethoven*. At the height of the film there's a remarkably perceptive conversation between the mother and the father. The father is all consumed by his dream of work at the expense of his family. It takes his wife to bring a new perspective to his life. She reminds him that while he's preoccupied with his personal dreams, his family's going down the drain.

Then there's the film, *Hook*, which is about a Dad who never has any time for his children, but ends up as a hero. People who watch the film want the father in the film to be warm and affectionate towards his children, but they know that in real life, this is just a dream.

For christians, it can't remain a dream. Fathers must make time available for their children. I build into my diary time for my children. Every month I try to spend some time alone with each of them and it's wonderful to see their reaction. 'This is my time with Dad' they think. 'You three aren't coming because it's Dad and me on our own!'

Fatherhood is at the very heart of God and He reveals Himself as our Father throughout His Word. It strikes me that He often sees me in the same way as I see my children. I'm aware of my shortcomings as a father, but I know that I can ask Him for strength, wisdom and common sense. And as I read His Word, I find that it's full of helpful guidance on raising children in an ungodly society such as ours. If we ignore the Bible, we're courting disaster.

Many people have very little understanding of human fatherhood and consequently have a wrong view of the fatherhood of God. We may not be able to go back and change the mistakes we've made in the past, but we can move forward and make godly fatherhood a priority in our children's lives. I appeal to married couples, seek God about the role of the father because it's crucial. There's a generation out there that has almost no example to follow. It's up to the people of God to demonstrate a radical concept of fatherhood. We shouldn't be ashamed of what we believe, or opt out. We need to take our responsibility seriously and father our children by the grace of God.

CHAPTER 19

Liz talks about the role of the mother

I am a trained nurse and have enjoyed many different kinds of responsibility and challenges in my job. I always found nursing very fulfilling and wondered how I would manage when I gave up work to become a mother at home.

It is a whole new world! I have found motherhood to be the greatest challenge — the most responsible job I have ever been given; the most demanding task I have ever undertaken and the most fulfilling and rewarding calling of my life. In today's society there's a high expectation for women to continue with their careers immediately after having children. The pressure on women to return to work as soon as possible is so great that to choose to give up work to stay at home and just be a mother is considered to be a lesser position and, therefore, less fulfilling.

I have found that caring for four children from birth right through to their first day at school has been a full-time job in itself. I see it as a calling from God. He has entrusted me to raise my infants as He directs and I wouldn't expect anyone else to do it for me.

I have sometimes heard women say, 'I'm not a natural mother', or 'I feel I've lost my identity since I gave up work and stayed at home to be a mother'. Although some women do seem to take more naturally to motherhood than others, we all need to find our resources in God and not just in our natural ability. I have found that natural ability very quickly runs out with a tempestuous two year-old!

At the heart of any struggle with motherhood is our common enemy — selfishness. Jesus said, 'Whoever finds his life will lose it, and whoever loses his life for my sake will find it' (Matt. 10:39). Being a mother is a great way to learn how to become a disciple of Jesus. My own mother, who died before she could see any of my children, was a great example of selfless love. Although I was never spoilt, she loved me in such a caring giving way that I can now appreciate and see the influence that she had on my life.

What you are and how you interact with your children will have a great part to play in shaping and moulding their lives. It sounds more like a high calling than a second class position, wouldn't you say?

MOTHER BY EXAMPLE

Your children are constantly observing and copying your behaviour. If you raise your voice, so will they; if you swear, so will they; if you lack self control, don't expect them to exercise it. Paul says that younger women need to be trained to love their husbands and children, to be self controlled and pure, to be busy at home, kind and to be subject to their husbands (Titus 2:4,5).

There's nothing like having four children under the age of eight to put your self control to the test. In my own strength I failed miserably, but again we need to realise we have a great resource — the Holy Spirit. If we ask Him to fill us and learn to let Him direct us, we will bear His fruit, one of which is self control.

YOUR RELATIONSHIP WITH YOUR HUSBAND

Paul mentions loving our husbands and being subject to them. How you love and respect your husband will largely determine how your children will respond to him. If you are negative and quick to criticise your husband in front of your children, if you are always pointing out his weaknesses, this will influence what they think of him.

Our love for each other as husband and wife and our mutual respect and honouring of each other, will bring our children stability and security. As they see a demonstration of love, devotion, commitment, respect and submission in the home, they will put on these attitudes themselves and take them into life.

A DEMONSTRATION OF LOVE AND ENCOURAGEMENT

Although we readily agree that we love our children, we may not be so quick to express what we are feeling. Children need constantly to be affirmed and told that they are loved. I make a point of telling them at some time every day that I love them and of showing that love with physical affection. The loving caress of a mother isn't just for tiny babies, it's for all your children while they're growing up. Let me encourage you to show them your love often. Kiss them, put your arms round them, hold them tight and express your love for them. Tell them how much you care about them and enjoy helping them as they grow up. Give them plenty of praise and encouragement and point out specific areas of progress you see them making. This all sounds rather obvious, I know. But when your children are with you 24 hours a day and at the stage when they need constant instruction and correction, it's easy to miss the opportunity to be positive and give them encouragement.

As they get older and become increasingly aware of themselves and how they relate to their peers at school, they will need your involvement, advice and encouragement. So take an interest in how they look, help them with their clothes, teach them about hygiene and express to them how lovely they are even if you are biased! This all helps to build into them confidence and a good self image.

Our eldest daughter is now at secondary school studying for her G.C.S.E.s. It's a girls' school and she's the only christian in her class. When she has chosen to walk a totally different path from others, she has met with hostility. Initially she was ridiculed for not going with the crowd — not swearing, gossiping, going out late to discos and drinking, or sleeping with a boyfriend. But as time has gone by she has earned respect and trust and is often taken into people's confidence when they have a problem.

The pleasures and temptations she has faced, she has been able to chat through with me — often late at night sitting on her bed. This didn't happen suddenly. Communication started when she was very young and has been continually worked at over the years. It often happens at the most inconvenient time, but it really is the key to having a successful relationship with your children. Don't ever be too busy not to notice when someone small wants your attention. If you fail to respond too often, they'll stop coming to you.

The early years of consistent training, love and hard work really will build in character, security and stability. It will all pay off when they have to stand on their own in the world.

TRAINING CHILDREN TO SERVE

Have you noticed that children do not find it natural to serve? As I mentioned earlier, human nature is naturally selfish and if we feed our children's selfish desires by pandering to their needs we will produce selfish children.

Once David and I were in India having lunch with a family from a church in Goa. Their two grown-up children were at home and I was particularly impressed with the way they served and helped their mother without even being asked. When the children had gone, I remarked to the mother about this. She smiled, agreed that it had become second nature to them, but added that this had not always been the case. She had trained them from a very early age to help in the home — and they weren't all girls — two boys and one girl!

Initially, teaching our children to serve is painstakingly hard work. They probably won't do it as well as you do and it's quicker to do it yourself! But let us persevere. Not only will they be able to share the load, but our children will learn to be helpful and to look out for ways to serve. Then serving in the Kingdom of God will not be a foreign animal to them. And, by the way, do have a job plan because it won't happen by itself. It will need setting up and practical application.

CREATING A PEACEFUL ENVIRONMENT AT HOME

Home is a battleground in so many children's lives today. It is a place of tension, arguments and loneliness. Some of our two older children's friends are what is commonly termed, 'latch key kids'. They come home to an empty house after school and Mum and Dad sometimes don't get back until 7.00 p.m. In our society, if you call yourself a 'homemaker' you are regarded with scorn — 'Surely you've got something more important to do'.

While our children are young and vulnerable, being a homemaker is a vital role for the stability of family life. It is not just about doing housework! You create the atmosphere in your home. You make it a place of peace and a haven of security. You don't need lots of money, just be creative and put time into making it attractive. If it's a welcoming place, your children will want to be there and bring friends home.

Your lifestyle will reflect how things are at home. If you cram too much into your week, the atmosphere at home will become fraught because you will get behind with everything. Be wise in the way you use your time. Plan your week ahead, especially if you have small children at home because they will have needs.

Teach your children to have respect for the home. This may sound strange, but it's good to teach them to take care of things and put them away, and to have respect for other people's things and for their privacy. This all helps to create peace and order in the home and trains our children to behave well in other environments. I am amazed when some small child comes into our home, empties every toy box, walks over the toys and leaves a trail of havoc and destruction behind him! Expecting our older children to keep their bedrooms tidy, means training them to put their toys away when they're a lot younger!

Family times together are an invaluable part of home life. We tend to have our family get together over a meal. There we can relax together, eat and hold a family discussion. Depending on the ages of your children, the subject matter can be quite diverse and often very humorous. It's amazing what comes out once everyone gets going, and is often a sure way of finding things out — particularly what's happening in their lives.

I once read a newspaper article which stated that family meal times are over. To quote, 'Meal-times used to provide a sense of structure in the daily round. Home was where most people ate, usually at pre-ordained times. Now fewer and fewer families eat any sort of cooked meal together, much less sit round a table for it, even on a Sunday, and half the population watches television while eating or eats on the hoof'.

The tragedy here is not so much people's eating habits — although they leave much to be desired — but the fact that families are not having any communication or life together as a family unit. Let's risk being called 'old fashioned' when we are trying to be biblical. Let's not be afraid to declare that we're homemakers and to give ourselves fully to the responsibilities that God has given us as mothers.

One last thing — we must let our children go. We don't own them. God has given them to us for a season. He wants us to train them to become mature and independent, able to stand on their own and be effective for Him.

I have many friends who have had to cut emotional ties with their mothers. I don't want my children to feel that they must come and see me out of a sense of guilt or duty, but because they want to.

We are not perfect. We make lots of mistakes in bringing up our children. But we can put our faith and trust in God for them and that will help us release them into what He has for their lives.

CHAPTER 20

Building a spiritual environment

How do we build a spiritual environment for our children? I'll give you three guidelines in this chapter and some more in the last two.

SET A GENUINE EXAMPLE

If you pray, your children will pray. If you read the Bible, so will they. If you worship, they'll worship. If you go round the house singing songs, they'll do the same. If you speak in tongues it's going to be just as natural to them to speak in tongues when they're filled with the Spirit. If you demonstrate the fruit of the Spirit, they'll be loving, joyful, peaceful, and so on. If you want a spiritual environment, then you've got to be spiritually active.

BE NATURAL

You don't need to do religious things to create a sort of spiritual atmosphere in your home. There's no secular/spiritual divide. God is involved in every area of our lives, so we should be spiritually natural and naturally spiritual all the time.

A few years ago a book came out that talked about the need for a family altar. I wondered if that was about child sacrifice! But it was actually referring to the need for families to come together once a day for some kind of spiritual connection. In our home we pray together most days, but that's not the only time when we include God. If one of the children hurts his finger in the evening when you had your spiritual time in the morning, you don't ignore this. You stop everything, get all the other children together, lay hands on the person who's hurt and pray. I'm after a spiritual atmosphere in which God is relevant all day long.

This sort of spirituality is natural for a child. Sometimes, as I've gone upstairs, I've overheard one of our children praying for another to be healed. It's hilarious. 'In the name of JESUS!' they pray. Where do they get that from? You. They just copy what you do — and hopefully they get better results! Whatever happens, they're being naturally spiritual — and that's the way I want it to be.

For this to run smoothly, it's a good idea to have a time when you can be together. We meet at 7.30 a.m. — which means that everyone has to be at the breakfast table by them. We spend a short time reading Scripture and praying for one another's needs. Then we worship God. We often get really excited when we do that. It has been known for us to be dancing round the front room at 7.45. I don't know what the passers-by think when they look in. They probably think we're crazy. For us, it's all natural.

A friend of mine told me, 'We just can't get the family together to pray. We just never have that opportunity.' I replied, 'Well we manage it, so why can't you?' I told him what we did and he said, 'We just couldn't do that'. The discussion ended there.

You have to decide one way or the other. Either you have a time together with God or you don't. Whether it's morning, afternoon or evening, if you do have one, you must be consistent. I think that a family benefits from a set time of family prayer coupled with more occasional prayer times. Whatever you decide to do, make sure that Jesus is real not just on Sundays, or for half an hour each day, but right the way through the week.

INSTRUCT

If you want a good spiritual atmosphere in your home you'll instruct your family and encourage your children to walk with God. You'll tell them about God, about His world, about what He's doing today, about His church, about the future and about how to handle pressures. Orthodox Jewish parents really follow through with Psalm 78:1–8. They continually pass on things about God to their children — it's so challenging. We should be doing the same — explaining doctrines about God and talking about the way He deals with us. At school they have to put up with negativism all day, so at home we can tell them about what's positive.

Your children will ask you difficult questions. You'll pray for them to be healed and they won't be healed. Then they'll say, 'Why hasn't God healed me?' From here you'll get involved in a conversation all about healing. Our children are fascinated by heaven and eternal life and they'll ask us about that. Then there's evolution. One of our children has a teacher who's convinced that the Bible is a set of fairy stories and this will lead our family into a discussion on the authority of Scripture. Every day I find myself instructing my children about the Word of God. I'm often talking to them about God's character and what He's doing. I want to be available to them and to instruct them in everything I know.

The subject of sex doesn't wait until senior school any more. It makes an appearance when children are seven or eight years old. You need to know when to speak to them and what to say. The truth will set people free. If you don't know the Word of God yourself, then you'll never be able to give accurate answers to the questions your children ask. If you're saturated in the Word of God, you'll have tremendous wisdom and will know what to say.

Is your home a place where Jesus is relevant to everyday life? Charismatic churches are in great danger of surviving on good meetings. It's not enough and it won't work in the end. Your home needs to have a spiritual environment and that comes when you set an example, when you're spiritually natural and when you instruct your children from the Word of God.

CHAPTER 21

Communication

A nother way to create a good atmosphere for your children is through communication. When a young person becomes a teenager, he may think that he can't talk to his parents any more. The truth is that communication, or lack of it, began a long time before his thirteenth birthday. If you want to communicate with your teenage children, you've got to start when they're much younger. You've got to talk a great deal and continually express what's going on inside you.

When your children are two, three or four years old you must enter into their world. I could write in my diary, 'Spend time with Julia'. That could mean me sitting in front of the television watching the cricket and our having the following conversation: 'Dad'. 'Yes'. 'Dad'. 'Yes'. 'DAD!' This isn't communication. Communication is stopping everything else that I'm doing and entering into Julia's world.

The most important thing isn't the length of time you spend with your children, it's the quality of that time. You can enter their world for just five minutes and they'll be over the moon. Sometimes I'll sit on the side of their bed with them in the evening. They think it's wonderful. I'm getting down to where they are and communicating in their world. You just watch their response as you communicate with them.

Your communication must be two way. That's not the norm. Usually Dad comes home from a busy day, sits down with his family at the meal table and the following conversation ensues, 'How was school today?' 'OK.' 'Did you learn anything new?' 'No.' 'Did anything special happen?' 'Ughh!' End of conversation. I don't let conversations go on like that. I want them to know that I'm interested in what happened to them at school today. So I look them in the eyes and I communicate that. It takes time and that time reflects my priorities.

If you're too busy to communicate with your children, you must change your priorities. As I mentioned earlier, Liz and I sit down with our diaries at the beginning of every month and go through every day of that month. We discuss what we're going to do, when we need babysitters and whether I've booked us into too many things. We work out when we're going to spend time with the children and when we're going to take each of them out. We talk it all through; it seems the obvious thing to do.

BE AVAILABLE

If you want to show your children that you're available to them, you must take an interest in their interests. You might think that what they're doing is dull, stupid and childish, but you must still be interested. They'll come up to you and say, 'Look what I drew at school today'. You know that you're supposed to know immediately what it is, but all you can see is some scribble. It would be easy for you to say, 'Oh that's nice, dear'. But this sort of comment is very hurtful. You need to ask them what it is and enter their world. It's so much more helpful for them. You also need to take an interest in what they're supposed to be interested in — which is probably homework.

In his book on raising children, Zig Ziglar says, 'the saddest words in the English Language, when it comes to raising children are these "if only."' That's so powerful. Billy Graham was once asked, 'If you could live your life again, what would you change?' He said, 'Two things. First, I wouldn't have gone to so many meetings, and second, I'd have spent a lot more time with my children because they grew up so quickly'. If a great man of God says that, we need to listen to him and make major adjustments in our lifestyle.

TURN OFF THE TELEVISION

The television is a major obstacle to family communication. Many families eat their evening meal in front of the television. I can walk down two or three roads in my neighbourhood and the television will be on in almost every house. It's the all-consuming passion and this generation of children are growing up with it — even though they're not always the ones who want to watch it. Families need to turn off the television and do things together — games or sports. The answer isn't just to get rid of the television, but to control the viewing.

Our children aren't allowed just to turn on the television. They have to ask, 'May I watch the television?' Sometimes we reply, 'No, you've had enough today'. At other times we say, 'Yes, of course you can. What are you going to be watching?' We take an interest in what's going on. One of the things the French can teach us is how to have a meal together. Their meals go on all evening — and the thinking behind them is this: the family around the dinner table communicating together.

The television mustn't control you, you must control it. What do you achieve by watching the television? Doesn't it destroy more than it achieves? It can ruin creativity, reading and conversation. Children copy their parents. If they don't read, it's probably because you don't. But if they often see you with a book, they'll start to read too. If they see you watching television all the time, you shouldn't be surprised if they do the same.

USE PHYSICAL CONTACT AND THE RIGHT WORDS

An important part of communication is physical contact. Liz has already touched on that — hugging, kissing, eye contact. Someone once said, 'You never know when a moment and a few sincere words can have an impact upon a life for ever'. That's so powerful. People say, 'I've never forgotten what my Dad said to me when I was six. It hurt me so much.' If that's true of negative words, it must also be true of positive ones. I'm going to speak words of comfort, strength, confidence and love that will last all the way through my children's lives.

BUILD MEMORIES

When your children are older you want them to look back on lives that are full of wonderful memories. You need to build these memories in while they're still young. Sometimes the most memorable moments happen spontaneously. You don't have to wait for them. You just build them into your lifestyle.

Liz and I don't just rely on holidays to give our children memories. It's tragic when the only memorable times you can remember were when you were on holiday. No, we deliberately plan things that we can do with our children in order to create memories for them. We want them to remember things that happen during every week — and they don't have to cost a lot of money.

One year we were fortunate enough to go to Orlando. We visited Disneyworld, had 'Back to the Future' rides — the whole works. It was great, but it cost money. Our children are just as happy going for a walk or a bike ride. So don't think that you've got to spend loads of money building good memories into your children's lives. Just plan simple things knowing that your children will treasure these memories for the rest of their lives. It may sound obvious, but do ensure that you build in time later on to talk through those memories. 'Do you remember that day when ...?' is guaranteed to have everyone taking part in the conversation.

CHAPTER 22

Guarding children from the world

The right environment for children must be a protected environment. How do we guard our children from the world? Jesus says that we're 'not of the world' (John 17:16), but we're certainly in it. There are two extremes on this subject. First, you can go ridiculously over the top and fiercely protect your children from the world — which will eventually make them rebellious. And second, you can totally neglect your children — not caring what television programmes or videos they watch. You need to draw a line right down the middle of these two approaches.

Parents ask me what I think about *Ghostbusters*. The next year they question me about *Teenage Mutant Ninja Turtles* and the year after that, they want to know my opinion of *Jurassic Park*. If I make a major issue out of these things, they'll be no end to it. So what I usually say is, 'They come and they go'. The best policy is to fill the children's lives with something that's a realistic alternative.

The greater problem that parents have with all the latest crazes isn't the craze itself, but all the packaging that goes with it. Every year you have to change the lunch boxes or the track suit! If you go along with this, you're very foolish. It's all about money and I belittle the whole thing with my children. So don't make a big issue out of it and get all spiritual, but don't trivialise it either. Just let your children know that you understand, but refuse to go along with it.

Some parents are obsessed by the need for their little child to wear the latest type of track suit — because all the other children will have one. Why not say to your child, 'You can be different. You don't have to have one.' Wow! What an amazing revelation — you can be different! I tend to let the latest rages take their course.

Sometimes the greater problem isn't so much the latest craze as a more subtle activity. Take the increase in the number of New Age children's television programmes for example. They're weird. Liz and I talk about them to our family, but we don't go overboard. We want to guard our children from the media, but we need to get where they are and talk it through with them. Then we can work out a solution. Of course, if something's obviously wrong, we'll declare it to be wrong.

Peter Meadows, whom I think was a consultant at Bridgehead Communications, once spoke at a conference I attended. He said that he'd gone to a video shop and had taken out a PG video for his children to watch. He put it on and went into the next room with his wife. After a while, one of the children interrupted him. 'Dad' he said. 'If you knew what we were watching next door you wouldn't believe it.' Peter went to check out the video and discovered his children watching a nude scene. Apparently at the beginning of the film were some trailers of films which were coming up in the future. One of these was mistakenly labelled PG when it was actually an 18 certificate. He wrote to the people concerned and explained the situation. They were terribly sorry and said that although the video had been out for a year, he was the first parent in the whole country to complain about it. We must guard our children from the media.

Censorship has become an increasingly controversial issue for christians anyway. *Jurassic Park* is rated PG. The first 45 minutes is all about scientists discussing how to recreate dinosaurs. I can't understand much of it, so how a three year-old could cope beats me! The second half of the film is quite terrifying and there's no way you could let young children watch it. Even Spielberg himself wouldn't let his eight and ten year-old children see it. When parents are not sure about a film, they ought to watch it before they decide whether their children should see it — even if this does mean two lots of tickets. PG (Parental Guidance) has got to mean just that.

GLAD TO BE AT HOME?

Do you love being in your home or are you longing to get away from it? Do you think, 'Oh great I'm at home!' or, 'Oh no! How can I get away again?' Your answer depends on the sort of home environment that you've created. If your house is always in chaos, noise and confusion, you need to do something about it. You must make sure that you create the right environment so that you can raise your children according to God's principles.

CONCLUSION

The most important thing of all is that the Bible works. We have a choice: either we take God at His Word, or we go along with the crowd. Christians should stand out from the crowd. We'll be laughed at and ridiculed, but it's the fruit that counts in the end. Some parents will simply read about raising their children God's way. Others will read and make every effort to put the teaching into practice. Jesus said that those whose lives are built on sand merely hear the Word, but that those whose lives are built on rock — the solid foundation of life — hear the Word and do it. Everybody knows that the atmosphere of raising children can be likened to the height of a raging storm — where do you go, who do you turn to, are you getting it right? What's the foundation of your family life — sand or rock?

Be determined. If raising children is on God's heart, do it His way and you'll find that it works. The truth will set you free! The choice is yours. Welcome to the unpredictable adventure of raising children who will make a difference in their generation both today and tomorrow.